HOW TO
RESOURCE YOUR
VISION

By Dick Edic

HOW TO
RESOURCE YOUR VISION

By Dick Edic

ISBN: 978-1-61529-042-0

Published by:

Vision Publishing
1079 Main Street E 109
Ramona, Ca 92065
(760) 789-4700

www.booksbyvision.com

HOW TO RESOURCE YOUR VISION

What Christian Leaders Are Saying

"As president of a distance-learning bible education institution, I have found this to be the most comprehensive and affordable church stewardship ministry training program available. We will be offering a tailored version, for credit, to our thousands of Learning Centers and churches around the world." -- *Dr. DeKoven, President, Vision International College/University*

"Two thumbs up! Pastors and church leaders will not regret ordering this (book). Finally, there is a comprehensive source of materials to maximize financial teaching and generosity in local churches." -- *Rev. Brian Kluth, Former Senior Pastor, Author/Speaker on Generosity, Past President of Christian Stewardship Association*

"Here is strong help for the pastor who longs to have an energized and growing congregation. We do a great injustice to the people we serve when we do not allow stewardship to have a central position in our teaching and program." -- *Dr. Bob Ricker, Former President, Baptist General Conference*

"You have achieved a major accomplishment that will be of great value to churches throughout the nation. Congratulations on your excellent effort." -- *Charles Schultz, J.D. President, Crescendo Interactive, a planned giving software compan*

"I highly recommend this material to pastors and lay leaders who desire to make stewardship a key component of discipleship. Funding a church's vision is often the missing piece in achieving fruitful results." -- *Dr. Jerry Sheveland, President, CONVERGE (Baptist General Conference)*

"This material is an important resource to those who share the growing realization of how important stewardship education and training are within the local church." -- *Dick Towner, Vice President, Good Sense Ministry, formerly a ministry of Willow Creek Association*

"A Complete Guide" -- *Dr. Scott M. Preissler, Former President, Christian Stewardship Association*

"I highly recommend (this book) and Vision Resourcing Group as an excellent training process that will enable our churches to teach their people biblical and practical stewardship." -- *Dr. Mike Livingston, District Superintendent, Western District Missionary Church*

"Do you want your people to manage their resources God's way, including living a generous life? (This book) and Vision Resourcing Group can help you accomplish just that."-- *Howard Dayton, CEO & Founder of COMPASS – Finances God's Way*

ACKNOWLEDGEMENT

I am thankful to the Executive Management Team and the Board of Overseers of the Baptist General Conference (now CONVERGE), years ago, for granting me the sabbatical months to complete my initial book, *Resourcing Your Vision – A Church Stewardship Training Guide*. I appreciate their commitment to the priority of teaching Christians biblical stewardship and generosity. I want to give a special thanks to Dennis Smith, my former-boss, now retired, as vice president of Baptist General Conference Ministry Partner Services, who years ago agreed with me that this was important and worth the long-term effort. He spent many hours with me in discussing the project and actually writing some initial drafts. I also want to thank the colleagues and organizations mentioned throughout this book that provided much of the content and chapters. I appreciate the opportunity I had to implement a "Stewardship/Generosity Ministry" at College Ave. Baptist Church in San Diego, California, my home church at the time. Thank you to Tom and Emily Barton, my original editors, and Kathy Smith, my current one. Your help and suggestions were invaluable. And thank you Desiree Sullivan, for your great art work on my book covers. Her website is www.DesireeLSullivan.com." Thank you.

Most of all, I am grateful to my wonderful Lord Jesus, whose Spirit within me has motivated and directed me in teaching biblical stewardship truths, and in the writing of this book. I pray that it will be used by God to motivate the reader to seek help in implementing their own tailored "Stewardship/Generosity Ministry" for their church, or in teaching this important subject mater to those people within their sphere of influence. May God be pleased and honored by the lives that will be changed as a result.

FORWARD

Having served as a senior pastor for 10 years, I experienced the challenge of motivating and teaching my congregation to understand and apply biblical principles of stewardship and generosity. Also as the past president of The Christian Stewardship Association, I also recognized the great need of church leaders to find ways and resources to teach their people biblical principles of money management along with expressing a more generous spirit. In fact, God eventually led me to go full-time in ministering my "Maximum Generosity" books, devotionals and website resources to church leaders around the world.

But these many years of experience in preaching and teaching biblical stewardship and generosity have made me realize that church leaders need more than bible studies, sermons, teaching outlines and seminars on different aspects of biblical stewardship and generosity. They need something more. First, they need a written guide on "why" and "how" to organize and implement a church stewardship and generosity ministry. They need to know how to find and train qualified leadership to implement and manage this important ministry to their congregation. They need to know which training resources are available, which ones to utilize and what fits the culture and maturity of their congregation. Second, in most cases, they will need some professional counsel and coaching in how to make it work and be successful. Even if a senior pastor and his staff desire to see this type of a ministry happen, experience has shown that most fail due to the lack of proper training and accountability. To use a computer analogy, they need an "operating system" and someone to train and guide them along while holding them accountable to stick with it, long-term, in order to realize success.

This book you are about to read, written by my good friend Dick Edic, is designed to provide you, first, with the reasons and motivation to implement a church stewardship & generosity ministry. You will need that motivation because it is a lot of work! It then tells you how to get started. It is practical, straight forward, and challenges you to go through a possible paradigm shift in thinking in how to really resource your church vision. Dick, with over 20 years of experience in church stewardship and generosity ministry training and implementation provides here a comprehensive guide, with selected resource material, to help you succeed. His passion has been to help God's people become free financially, walk more intimately with the Lord Jesus, and grow in generosity. And as a result of that generosity, both Dick and I want to see your church be fully resourced so that it, along with many others, can fund the Great Commission, reaching the world for Christ.

May God bless you and convince you to follow through with the teaching and motivation this book provides. And in years to come may you see a wonderful growth of your congregation in becoming better managers of what God has given them and more generous givers of that bounty.

Pastor Brian Kluth - Founder of www.MAXIMUMgenerosity.org and Bestselling Author of www.GenerousLife.org 30 & 40 Day Devotionals

Contents

INTRODUCTION

This book is a guide for motivating, training and equipping church and Christian leaders in **how to** develop a **culture** of biblical stewardship and generosity to those people within their sphere of influence. It is directed primarily to pastors and church leaders, since that is where stewardship and generosity should be taught. However, the principles and "process" taught here can certainly be applied within the context of a Christian school or business environment. You may be a school leader that wants to help your staff, students and donors grow in their application of biblical stewardship and generosity. Or, you may be a Christian business person who wants to help your staff and employees benefit personally from this teaching. We know that stress from financial problems affects motivation and productivity in the work place. You would surely agree that our young people certainly need to learn these important principles before they enter into the challenges of adult life.

The big question is how does a Christian leader organize and implement a strategy, or "process" in his or her organizational environment? How does he/she effectively utilize the multiple resources for teaching stewardship, money management and generosity to those people within his/her sphere of influence, whether it be a church congregation, school, or business?

Because the church is where this important teaching should start, the **major focus** of this book is to help pastors and church leaders learn ways to empower and motivate their congregations toward a greater generosity and intimacy with God. Even if you are a Christian business or school leader, chances are you are also a church leader in some capacity. Chances are, along with your pastor, you want to be able to resource the God-given vision for your church. Although my primary goal is to see pastors and church leaders equipped in training others to become more generous givers and faithful managers of God's resources, many of the principles and resources mentioned in this book can be utilized within the environment of a business or school. So, take and apply those principles and truths contained in this book that work for your particular church or organization. You'll find out what works for you. And don't hesitate to seek help from the resources mentioned later in the book. Chances are you will need it and want it in order to succeed.

I've designed the book to help the reader understand the "**what**", "**why**", and "**how**" to accomplish this goal. Because of the magnitude of this goal, and the space limitations within a single book, the focus will be on the "**what**" and "**why**", with some *general* instructions, principles, and resources provided in the "**how**". In Chapter Six, Appendix One and Two, I direct you to additional resources and help beyond the scope of this book, some of it *free.*

By the time you finish reading and digesting the truths contained in this book, assuming that you are serious about the subject, you should be motivated and encouraged to move ahead in helping your church, school, or business entity develop a culture of biblical stewardship, money management and generosity. And regarding the image of the **water faucet** on the cover, you will learn its meaning in Chapter One.

Our contributors to this book have many years of combined experience in some aspect of stewardship and generosity ministry leadership and training. You will be hearing from the best. BUT, be prepared to possibly go through a **paradigm shift!** We won't be talking about just another stewardship campaign, fund-raising effort, bible study, or seminar. You may be surprised!

CHAPTER ONE –

WHAT?

Let's start with **"*What* do <u>you</u> want?"** Think this through carefully and honestly. Match your answers to this list of possible "wants":

- I just want to meet budget.
- I want to increase the salaries and benefits of the staff.
- I want to pay off existing debt.
- I want to improve the church facilities.
- I want our church to support more missionaries.
- I want our church to be instrumental in transforming our members to become conformed to the image of Christ and become generous as Christ is generous.

Which ones match yours? Which one is your top priority? Obviously, all are valid "wants" in God's eyes, but what does He want for you?

What does <u>God</u> want? Would you agree that the last bullet above is His top priority for your people? What would happen to the other "wants" if that one was your top priority? Here are a few biblical passages describing God's heart regarding your people:

- "The people are bringing more than enough for doing the work the Lord commanded to be done....And so the people were *restrained* from bringing more, because what they already had was more than enough to do all the work." (Exodus 36: 5 & 6b-7).
- "Now, who is willing to consecrate himself today to the Lord?....The people rejoiced at the willing response of their leaders, for they had given freely and whole-heartedly to the Lord." (1 Chronicles 29:5b & 9)
- "Do not store up <u>for yourselves</u> treasures on earth, where moth and rust destroy, and where thieves break in and steal. But store up <u>for yourselves</u> treasures in heaven....for where

your treasure is there your heart will be also….No one can serve two masters. Either he will hate the one and love the other, or he will be devoted to the one and despise the other. You cannot serve both God and Money." (Matthew 6:19-24)

- "And now, brothers, we want you to know about the grace that God has given the Macedonian churches. Out of the most severe trial, their overflowing joy and their extreme poverty welled up in rich generosity….But just as you excel in everything – in faith, in speech, in knowledge, in complete earnestness and in your love for us – see that you also excel in this grace of giving." (2 Corinthians 8:1-2, 7)

- "Command those who are rich in this present world not to be arrogant nor to put their hope in wealth, which is so uncertain, but to put their hope in God, who richly provides us with everything for our enjoyment. Command them to do good, to be rich in good deeds, and to be generous and willing to share. In this way they will lay up treasure <u>for themselves</u> as a firm foundation for the coming age, so that they may take hold of the life that is truly life." (1 Timothy 6:17-19)

In light of what God is telling you in these few passages listed above, be thinking and asking yourself, "Just how am I going to help my people become like those expressed in these passages as well as described below by some Christian leaders?"

What do Christian <u>leaders</u> say? Here are some *comments* from Christian leaders about the *priority* of seeking to influence the transformation of your people to become conformed to the image of Christ, developed into mature biblical stewards, and become generous as Christ is generous. Some of these quotes are taken from the excellent book "Revolution in Generosity – Transforming Stewards to be Rich Toward God", Wesley K. Willmer, Editor, Moody Publishers:

- "Our approach to money and possessions isn't just important – it's central to our spiritual lives. Our giving is a reflexive response to the grace of God in our lives. It comes out of the transforming work of Christ in us….Stewardship isn't a subcategory of the Christian life. Stewardship is the Christian life." (Randy Alcorn – *author of* Money, Possessions and Eternity, *and* The Treasure Principle)

- "Money is integral to life. It reflects who we are and what we value. If we are to worship God, this worship must include our finances. Unfortunately, many ministries today overlook this important truth." (Robert Wuthnow, Andlinger *Professor of Sociology and Director of Center for the Study of Religion, Princeton University*)

- "In order for Christians to better serve the Lord, they must become free from financial bondage. The road to freedom begins when God's people apply His principles of handling money to their personal finances. *The church needs to help them learn and apply these principles."* (The late Larry Burkett, founder of *Christian Financial Concepts* and past Chairman of the Board of *Crown Financial Ministries.*)

- "We need to train people to be financially faithful in order to know Christ more intimately and to be freed to serve Him." (Howard Dayton, chief executive officer of *Compass – Finances God's Way* & former *co-founder of Crown Financial Ministries)*

- "The lack of biblical stewardship has reached a crisis level in America. At the root of this crisis is a lack of discipleship, which calls us to revisit the meaning of biblical stewardship. If we are to accomplish our God-given vision to be a 'movement of Great Commission Christians who are glorifying God by building Christ's Church worldwide,' we must relearn the scriptural principles that guide earning, spending, saving and giving." (The Christian & Missionary Alliance Church "Executive Summary" speaking about *Stewardship and the Kingdom of God)*

- "Few people are born givers. For some, being a generous giver is a gift from God; for others, it was learned from parents who modeled tithing. For most, though, giving grows because of what church leaders do, and do not do, to help people learn what it means to give." (Donald W. Joiner, in his book *Creating a Climate for Giving)*
- "There is a tremendous need for churches today to educate and assist people with managing their resources in God-honoring ways...a stewardship ministry can be used by God to remove a major stumbling block to spiritual growth and development. When money is no longer the chief rival god, when money no longer controls the person but the person controls money, and when the deceitfulness of riches is exposed and can no longer choke out God's word (Matthew 13:22), individuals are freed up to relate to God and to serve God in profoundly new and deeper ways." (Dick Towner, Vice President, *Good $ense Ministry*, formerly a ministry of Willow Creek Association*)*
- "This is key: Pastors of local churches must see stewardship education as part and parcel of Christian discipleship." (J. David Schmidt, in his book, *Choosing to Live: Financing the Future of Religious Body Head-quarters)*
- "As we enter the 21st century, we are witnessing the confluence of two sweeping currents – the unprecedented accumulation of evangelical wealth in America and the unparalleled opportunity for the growth of the Church around the world. We believe that these two trends have not met by coincidence, but by providence... As of today, the harvest is undercapitalized. Research tells us that the funds exist in abundance...they just need to be redirected to further His Kingdom." (Daryl Heald, Past President of *Generous Giving*, in his booklet "Imagine A Revolution...A Revolution Of Generosity,")

Do the comments above reflect your heart for your church or organization and the people you influence? Could you use some help in getting there? To start with the *church,* let me help you have a clearer image of what a church would look like having implemented a "Stewardship/Generosity Ministry" as described above. Here is what it would look like:

What **are the** *attributes* **of a** <u>**biblically generous church?**</u> These attributes can also apply to a business or school environment. This list is taken from the author's experience and *Generous Church* website, a great place to learn more.

- **Biblical stewardship and generosity are seen as** *whole life issues,* not just raising money for the budget. It involves people's *time, talent & treasure.* Members are taught about the importance and effective deployment of spiritual gifts. Leadership models generous service in the church and community and encourages members to do the same.

- **The concept of biblical stewardship is woven into the culture and values of the church.** It is a core value of the church. The Senior Pastor and other church leaders are comfortable teaching and modeling biblical stewardship and generosity. Stewardship related information is provided from many ministry "areas" around the church, including its web site. The congregation is familiar with the financial state of affairs of the church.

- **Stewardship has strong support from church leadership.** Stewardship is a recognized and distinct ministry within the church, and the church budgets money needed to achieve its goals. There is strong prayer support for this ministry when all church ministries and departments partner with their efforts.

- **Stewardship/generosity is taught consistently from all ministries of the church.** Leadership seeks to understand the level of congregational understanding of biblical and practical principles of stewardship and generosity. The congregation has a high level of understanding and application of these truths.

- **Stories of successful management and generosity are shared regularly at church events and worship services.** Stewardship and generosity emphasis are part of worship services, especially when it is not "budget time" or an expressed need.

- **Generous lifestyles are lived throughout the leadership and congregation.** A significant number of the congregation gives generously of their time as volunteers in their church. There is an overall attitude of cheerfulness in giving throughout the church.

- **There is a designated stewardship leader to champion the cause of biblical generosity throughout the church.** The church has a staff member or lay volunteer stewardship/generosity ministry leader with a lay team in place and dedicated to facilitate the stewardship vision of their church. The stewardship/generosity ministry leadership team has clearly defined roles and responsibilities…and has the FULL support of the senior pastor and leadership of the church.

- **A well-developed stewardship/generosity ministry strategy and agenda is in place.** This agenda is aligned with the church master calendar and supported by the church staff. This also includes a system for measuring their progress and success.

- **Stewardship and biblical generosity are taught as part of the teaching and training of the church.** Teaching programs and events are scheduled throughout the years from all ministries, departments and for all age groups.

- **The results of the above are that church needs are abundantly met.** There is no need to repeatedly pressure the congregation to give more or hold fund-raising campaigns every few years. Giving to missions increases. Giving to the poor increases. Consumer debt held by members is reduced. God is glorified!

Which attributes listed above reflect your church or organization? How much would you like to see your church (or business or school) experience these qualities? Let's pause for a moment and let me give my (and many others) *definition* of a "stewardship/ generosity ministry" (or "process") within a church, business or school environment:

> *It is a comprehensive training "process" that takes biblical and practical stewardship education into all areas of a church's ministries. It involves motivating and training members to manage their time, talent and treasure in such a way as to honor the God who gives them everything they have and are. I am emphasizing the word "ministry" rather than "campaign or event," because it implies an ongoing and long-term process. It means teaching whole-life management, not just tithing 10% to the church. It is everything a church plans, teaches, along with activities it implements annually to bring its membership to a full understanding of what a steward is. It is the process of bringing them to the ability level where they express this growing knowledge in actions that reflect submission to God's gracious leadership in their lives.*

Because your people are suffering from "information overload", your stewardship/generosity ministry or process needs to be holistic, communicating to them from many sources. **To use an analogy**, your ultimate goal is to get stewardship and generosity education into your church's or organization's ministry *"water system"* to insure that your people always get a "taste" of biblical stewardship and generosity at any ministry "faucet" they drink from (note the faucet image on this book cover). Some examples of ministry "faucets" are preaching, the offering during a worship service, Sunday-school teaching, small groups, school classroom teaching, lunch-time small group studies or workshops, new member orientation, seminars, children's ministries and church or organizational publications.

One of the outcomes of this stewardship/generosity ministry is generous giving in order to expand God's kingdom, resulting in more unbelievers worldwide being brought into a saving knowledge of Jesus Christ. God is honored and pleased by growing lives that reflect the life of Christ.

What **does it mean to "resource your vision"?** If the above reflects "success", what resources do you need to succeed? Because the look of "success" can vary, here is a partial list to consider:

- Well recruited, vetted and trained LEADERSHIP! As with all organizations, including churches, the right leadership for the job is imperative if you are going to succeed. Chances are you already have the right leadership candidates within your congregation or organization. In my "How" chapters, I'll give you some pointers on finding them.
- Trained TEACHERS to conduct the various classes, seminars and events on biblical and practical stewardship, money management God's way, and generosity. I will also discuss that in my "How" chapters along with resources in the two appendices.
- SEMINARS on multiple topics teaching basic debt reduction, budgeting, money management, generosity, financial and estate and charitable giving. I'll touch on some basic ideas on conducting successful seminars in my "How" chapters.
- SPECIAL EVENTS & CAMPAIGNS mixed in with your *educational* efforts to actually raise needed funds. I will tell you later where you can go for help.
- ESTATE & GIFT PLANNING, a very important capability, but mostly overlooked by churches. More on this later.
- COPY from multiple sources to include in various promotional and reporting venues. Some examples are a

church worship folder, annual or monthly reports and statements, newsletter, website, blogs, handouts etc. This keeps the message before your people. These include *teaching outlines, articles* on stewardship and generosity for your various communication pieces, *quotes* and *verses* on some aspect of stewardship and generosity.

- SOME OTHER stewardship/generosity ministry resources you could include. (Later I'll tell you how and where to access these resources):
    - A study that guides your people in discovering the life purpose that God intended for them. It gives them action steps to experience the life they were born to live in five major areas of life = Spiritual, Relational, Physical, Financial and Career.
    - How to implement a "Career Transition Ministry" that helps those in your congregation and community seeking a career change or job. This can be a great outreach opportunity for your church.
    - Small group study that teaches financial management, God's way. The study and its group dynamics change lives, such as God's part versus our part, debt reduction, budgeting, saving and investing, working effectively, and generosity.
    - Teaching your people biblical principles of ethics, enhancing their moral character and decision making process. It helps you develop a culture of integrity.
    - Teaching your leaders biblical principles of leadership strategies and skills. As mentioned above, in order to succeed in resourcing your vision, you *must* get quality *leaders* in the various departments and ministries of your church, business or school.
    - Generous giving resources available online to help your people grow in this important area of their lives. There are several excellent sources you can

use; some are a fun, interactive way to nurture a culture of generosity among your people.

- Testing resources to help you find the best people, at every level, to become a part of your lay-led stewardship/generosity ministry leadership team. They help you create effective teams and work groups by providing objective measurements and narrative reporting of group characteristics including interpersonal conflicts. This is very helpful in businesses and schools.
- A way to conduct volunteer and employee background screening as you develop your leadership teams and protect your church, business or school. This is also great for businesses and schools.
- A seminar designed to teach your people estate and gift planning, and how to make substantial gifts that are win-win for them and your church or school.
- A bible devotional hand-out that you can provide for your people that guides them in creating a spiritual journey to a more generous life. This can also be conducted in conjunction with a preaching series in your church.
- Access to local Christian foundations that can assist your people in placing specific planned gifts, such as securities, real estate, and art.
- Access to local, Christian, professional, financial and legal advisors who have been vetted and demonstrated professionalism and spiritual maturity. Once your people have been taught practical and biblical principles of money management, they will most likely need professional counsel on implementing their specific financial plan. Where do you find quality professionals with a biblical world-view to help them?

- Finally, maybe you need to provide advanced bible and leadership training to those lay leaders within your congregation who feel called to go to the next level in their spiritual and professional training for future ministry. There are some great resources available that allow your church to provide this on your own campus.

What are some *essential elements* of a successful Stewardship/ Generosity Ministry?:

- There should be a stated *vision* and *mission* that is shared by the leadership and members. You don't build a stewardship/generosity ministry on the budget. Does your church or organization have a *vision* and *mission* statement that is known and shared? If not, create one!
- The church or school should have a defined *ministry plan* that is understood and owned by the congregation and/or staff. This follows the *vision* and *mission* statement, and guides the stewardship/generosity ministry plan and agenda.
- The church or school should have a budget and funding plan that reflects *expected* outcomes and goals. These expected outcomes and goals come out of the church or school *ministry plan*. People need to see a funding plan that reflects "their" vision, mission and ministry plan in order to be motivated to support it. Long-term stewardship and generosity growth occurs as they participate in where the church or school is going and what it is about.
- The church or school should provide consistent stewardship/generosity teaching *at all levels and age groups*. This is very important! Do not treat this process as just another of the many ministries of the church or school. The effort must weave through *all of your ministries*. Remember the **analogy** of an organization's ministry "*water system*", where its people need to receive "tastes" of

this teaching from all the ministries, or "faucets" they encounter.

- *There must be strong* leadership commitment, both lay and staff. Without this, it will not happen, regardless of the interest of a few members of the church or school or business.
- The church or school leadership should have a *long-term* commitment. This is not a "quick fix." It must be part and parcel of the ongoing discipleship process. This is not a "fund-raiser," or "campaign," although it will definitely help bring about their possible success if implemented. Recognize that IT WILL TAKE TIME.
- The church or school must communicate a positive perception to its people of the benefits to them. They must not see it as just another way for the church or school to get more money from them. The focus needs to be that this is going to help them grow closer to God and experience the joy of giving and His intimate fellowship.

Keep in mind that your final stewardship ministry (or process) may look a little different than those for other churches or organizations. Final results will vary because although each church or organization may utilize many of the same activities and available resources, they may do them in a different sequence.

Here are some *observations* to guide you in implementing a Stewardship/Generosity Ministry:

- **The resources** for accomplishing God's vision for your church ministry are resident in the congregation. You may not think so, but when everyone practices good stewardship and generosity, your church will never lack resources. An example of this is a church I worked with several years ago. A study was conducted, and it was determined that if all of their households, or *giving units,* tithed their full 10%, the church budget could jump from $2 million per year to $15 million! Your church would probably experience a similar result.

- Other studies have shown that if everyone in a typical church congregation lived only on welfare, but *tithed* their welfare income, the church income would likely increase over what the church was receiving from their current giving!
- Churches that support global missions beyond themselves do not suffer at home. God will honor a church's faith to give outside their local ministry, such as supporting missions to unreached people groups.
- Fund-raising helps a cause and is short lived. A long-term stewardship/generosity ministry first helps the giver and then the cause of Christ - locally, nationally, and globally.
- Because this is a discipleship issue, giving is a good indicator of a person's spiritual condition. *In my opinion*, a pastor should know the giving records of his people. By so doing, he can spot potential spiritual problems and deal with them before it is too late. He would certainly want to know if a member of his congregation is involved in a moral sin, or was having marital or financial problems. He is their under shepherd, concerned for their well-being.

Here are some Do's and Don'ts of an Effective Stewardship/ Generosity Ministry

(Taken from a think tank report of experienced United Methodist clergy. For the reader seeking help for his or her business or school, apply what works for your organization)

...DO...

- ☺ Be bold and intentional (about your stewardship/generosity ministry).
- ☺ Don't hesitate to have an annual campaign (as well as a year-round approach).
- ☺ Promote tithing as the expectation (the starting point).

☺ Find appropriate (and personal) ways to say thank you to donors (absolutely!).

☺ Assign stewardship (ministry) to leaders, not the finance committee. ("apples" & "oranges")

☺ Provide stewardship (generosity) education for all age groups (especially your youth).

☺ Use Scripture to teach stewardship (foundational).

☺ Tell ministry stories about what contributions have made possible (people respond to stories).

...DON'T...

☹ Be apologetic or defensive about addressing stewardship. (Why would you do that?).

☹ Assume that people will understand their stewardship responsibilities without intentional communication. (They need to be patiently taught).

☹ Assume that people understand what the "tithe" means. (Most don't).

☹ Believe that the finance committee has the gifts to be stewardship (ministry) leaders.

☹ Communicate that stewardship is raising the budget every fall. (If you do, you will lose them)

☹ Overlook the offertory as a teachable moment for stewardship and generosity education and motivation. (This can be testimonies, quotes, or stories).

☹ Forget to tell (report) ministry stories in a variety of ways so that members understand what their contributions have made possible. (This will encourage them to give more).

☹ Report financial information to your members negatively or very often. (Don't beg or browbeat them to give).

☹ Put more energy into "Fall Harvest," silent auctions, church bazaars and other special events or gimmicks than you put into your ongoing stewardship program. (Show that you are really trusting God to motivate His people to give, not secular methods).

In his book, *Strategic Resource Development*, Jay Pankratz, Pastor of Rialto Community Baptist Church, Rialto, CA, lists *some myths and facts about ministry money*: (again, these truths can apply elsewhere)

Myth: If people receive much they will generously support those who gave to them.

Fact: If people serve more, they will give more. They need to demonstrate commitment.

Myth: It is unbiblical to state the specific amount that someone gives.

Fact: The Bible gives positive examples of people stating the amount of what was given to God. (1 Chron. 29:1-9; Acts 4:32-37; Mark 12:41-44) Leaders first, then congregation.

Myth: God's people should not sign a commitment card or make a vow.

Fact: God tells His people to make vows. (Psalm 50:14; 61:5; Rom. 10:9-10)

Myth: The more money you give to God, the more money you will get in return.

Fact: God usually rewards generosity with better things than money.

Myth: Financial giving does not affect our spiritual health, growth and blessing.

Fact: It is impossible to live by faith in God, love people and get God's full blessing while not being a generous giver to God's work. (Heb. 11:6)

Myth: One who is not giving generously can still be a good spiritual leader.

Fact: One who is not a generous giver will abuse spiritual leadership positions. (Luke 16:10-11)

Myth: Everyone should be challenged to give an equal amount, which represents his or her percentage of the congregation.

Fact: Everyone should make an equal and worthy sacrifice according to his or her wealth. Otherwise, the rich give too little and the poor feel guilty.

Myth: When the economy is down we should expect offerings to be down.

Fact: We should always trust God and seek to enlarge His work.

Myth: We should not ask people who are struggling financially to give to God.

Fact: People are often struggling because they are not giving to God, and God promises to provide for those who faithfully give to Him. (Phil. 4:10-19)

The goal of a good stewardship/generosity ministry is to move your people from "myth" to "fact," from wishing you could do God's vision to doing it because of their generous giving. Let these following **"giving statements"** become "facts" in your thinking and actions:

1. God is the source and giving is rooted in God, not affluent individuals, consultants, software, direct mail, etc.
2. The Bible provides the standard, which is the tithe, not "fair share," not "assessments," not "user fees."
3. Giving is indispensable to Christian discipleship. Raising funds is a spiritual ministry. It connects people with mission, prayers, gifts and service.
4. You have a right to be funded in your ministry, but you ought not claim your rights as much as express your thanks.
5. You should expect to raise 100% of your needs. Avoid "poor talk," whining, and negative attitudes; celebrate your victories.
6. Focus on the giver and not the money. The Christian disciple needs to give, regardless of his or her challenges or opportunities.

7. Emphasize your vision, not your financial need.
8. Giving includes more than the product of our labor. It is a volitional "heart" decision.
9. Giving involves friendship with the poor.
10. Giving moves beyond individual charity to building communities of interconnectedness, justice and compassion.

As I conclude this chapter, to be successful, it is not enough to have just some techniques, methods or events. You need to undergird your stewardship/generosity ministry activities with correct principles, concepts and philosophical understanding, or a "new" paradigm of thinking. Chances are that by the time you complete this book and embrace what is discussed and taught, you will have gone through a paradigm shift in how you approach your church or organizational budget and fund-raising.

When teaching stewardship and generosity, it is imperative that you start with the many truths mentioned above. Application of other aspects of stewardship, like giving, will not occur until the individual understands and yields to God's complete ownership of everything and their responsibility to manage God's resources. As Dr. Wesley K. Willmer, Executive Vice president of Evangelical Counsel for Financial Accountability and former Vice President of Advancement at BIOLA University, writes: "Stewardship is God's way of raising people, not man's way of raising money. God is working in us to help us become the people he wants us to be through how we learn to give. Stewardship is God's order for man's relationship to God, not man's relationship to an organization."

CHAPTER TWO –

WHY?

In chapter ONE, I talked about "WHAT?" Now, let's take a look at **"Why you should have a 'Stewardship/Generosity Ministry'"** or **"process"**. Answers to this key question will not only help motivate you to want it, but they will equip you in *persuading* your leadership team to want it.

How bad do you want to see your people become better stewards of their "time, talent and treasure?" Getting folks involved in resourcing your vision is a growing challenge in today's overwhelmed culture. Why are many churches and private schools *suffering* from a lack of adequate resources to fulfill their visions? Here are some **reasons**:

- The "demands" of affluence in our society.
- In our desire to "relate" to the "seeker," it is often unpopular to talk about money or ask for it.
- Because stewardship is not being taught that much in seminaries, many pastors are uneducated in biblical stewardship and, therefore, don't teach it to their business and school leaders.
- Some pastors, because of their own financial struggles and mistakes, feel hypocritical in addressing the topic.
- Because church members believe that they (rather than God) "own" their possessions, they are afraid to "let go" in generous giving, fearful of the "what ifs" of life.

Do any of the above apply to your church or organization? If so, consider yourself "normal." The **good news**, however, is that when properly taught biblical stewardship and generosity, including financial management, Christian's hearts can be transformed to be rich toward God and generous like Jesus. As a result they do grow and support the vision and mission of their church and/or non-profit organization. This has been true of many churches and schools that have implemented some form of a stewardship and generosity education effort.

Imagine what could happen in your church or organization if every one of your people became a generous giver of their time, talent and treasure? How would that affect the fulfillment of your vision? How would that look to have folks attending your church or organization that truly believed that all their possessions belonged to God, that they were merely managers (stewards), that they were experiencing peace because they knew their finances were in order with limited debt, that walked around with a joy in their heart because they were experiencing a generous heart and seeing God use them for His kingdom glory? How would that affect their productivity for your business enterprise?

Are you **dreaming**, or are you persuaded this could be a **reality?** I am assuming that because you care about the stewardship and spiritual "health" of your people, you are reading this book. You want to see your people give more of their finances and time. More importantly, you want to see your people grow into mature disciples of Christ, experiencing the joy of a more intimate walk with Him, and you want your church or organization to increase in its ability to help change the world locally, regionally and globally through changed lives.

Focusing now on pastors and church leaders, let's take a short quiz to help you get an idea of the stewardship/generosity "health" of your church, STOP HERE to **answer the following questions**. It's OK, no one will judge:
1. What is your average weekly attendance? _____
2. How many "households" does that represent? _____

_____

3. What is your church's average annual income? _____

4. Divide #3 by #2 to calculate the average giving per "household" _____

5. Estimate the *average* household annual income of your congregation _____

6. Divide #4 by #5 to calculate the average percent (%) giving of your people. _____%

7. <u>Here is an example</u>: 450 attendance, counting children = 260 "households". Church average annual income = $610,000 divided by 260 "households", or "giving units" = $2346 each. Divide $2346 by $78,000 average "household" annual income = 3% giving; which happens to be about the national average for evangelicals in the United States!

8. Another fact of math = If the giving people of this example church increase their average annual giving from 3% to 4%, as a result of a long-term stewardship/generosity education ministry, that equates to a 33% increase in the church's annual income!

9. Here is another question: How many funerals of your people have you had these past 5 years? _____

10. How much money came to your church as a result of their possible *bequests* or other planned giving of these estates?_____. If your answer is zero or very low, your church is among most other churches answering this question. We'll talk later in this book about including an estate/planned giving capability in your stewardship/generosity ministry.

11. Here are two concluding computations:

   a. If your people increased their giving by only 1%, how much more would come to your church budget? Compute this off the numbers you calculated above. Take the example above: 4% of $78,000 = $3120, an increase of $774, times 260 = $201,240 increase in giving to the church, divided by $610,000 original average income to the church = a 33% increase in giving to the church!

b. If your people increased their giving to a full tithe, or 10%, how would that look?: Taking the same example: $78,000 times 10% = $7800 times 260 households = $2,028,000 income to the church, an increase of $1,418,000, or 232%!

Well, how did you do? Discouraged? Don't be...**there is hope**. Now that you have a better understanding of the giving "health" of your congregation, where do you go now? If you did implement a stewardship/generosity ministry and your church income increased, what would you like to accomplish for God? List them here:

_____
_____
_____
_____
_____
_____
_____
_____
_____

Here are some examples of needs and dreams mentioned by other church leaders:

- Physical improvements to church facilities.
- Pay off existing debt.
- Add new staff.
- Increase salary and benefits to staff.
- Add more missionaries to support.

Because stewardship is not being effectively taught in our churches, biblical stewardship is the "silent" subject of Christianity. According to a Christian Stewardship Association/

Lilly Foundation survey years ago, stewardship is not being taught in our homes, colleges or in seminaries. Eighty five percent of pastors feel unequipped or afraid to teach this vital subject. Ninety percent of churches have no plan or program to train members in stewardship.

Here are some specific REASONS why you should have a stewardship/generosity ministry or process in your church or organization:

1. Let's start with **God's Word**. God commands spiritual leaders to teach, lead by example and encourage their people in the area of stewardship and giving. Take a look at these scripture passages:
   - **Moses** in Exodus 35:4-9, 20-24; 36:4-7 and Deuteronomy 8:11-18.
     Exodus 35:4-9 = "...This is what the Lord has commanded: From what you have, take an offering for the Lord. Everyone who is willing is to bring to the Lord an offering of..." *(God commands it)*
     Exodus 35:20-24 = "...and everyone who was willing and whose heart moved him came and brought an offering to the Lord for the work on the Tent of Meeting...All who were willing, men and women alike, came and brought gold jewelry of all kinds..." *(God wants us to be willing)*
     Exodus 36:4-7 = "The people are bringing more than enough for doing the work the Lord commanded to be done. Then Moses gave an order and they sent this word throughout the camp: 'No man or woman is to make anything else as an offering for the sanctuary.' And so the people were *restrained* from bringing more, because what they already had was more than enough to do all the work." *(Extravagant giving!)*
   - **King David** in 1 Chronicles 29:2-9 = "With all my resources I have provided for the temple of my

God…Besides, in my devotion to the temple of my God I now give my personal treasures of gold and silver for the temple of my God, over and above everything I have provided for this holy temple…Now who is willing to consecrate himself today to the Lord? Then the leaders of families, the officers of the tribes of Israel, the commanders of thousands and commanders of hundreds, and the officials in charge of the king's work gave willingly. ..The people rejoiced at the *willing response of their leaders*, for they had given freely and wholeheartedly to the Lord. David the king also rejoiced greatly." *(Leading by example leads to joyous results!)*

- **King Hezekiah** in 2 Chronicles 31:6-10 = "The men of Israel and Judah who lived in the towns of Judah also brought a tithe of their herds and flocks and a tithe of the holy things dedicated to the Lord their God, and they piled them heaps…When Hezekiah and his officials came and saw the heaps, they praised the Lord and blessed his people Israel. Hezekiah asked the priests and Levites about the heaps…and (they) answered, 'Since the people began to bring their contributions to the temple of the Lord, we have had enough to eat and plenty to spare, because the Lord has blessed his people, and this great amount is left over.'" *(God's ministers are provided for by "heaps" of giving!)*

- **Jesus in his Sermon on the Mount** provides a clear picture of the importance of stewardship and what our attitudes toward our possessions should be. He said in Matthew 6:21 and 24: "For where your treasure is, there your heart will be also" and, "No one can serve two masters. Either he will hate the one and love the other, or he will be devoted to the one and despise the other. You cannot serve both God and money." *(What is your real 'treasure'? That's where your heart is. Unfortunately too many Christians are serving the 'god' of money.)*

- The **Apostle Paul,** in 2 Corinthians 8 & 9, presented the Macedonian church as a wonderful example of biblical stewardship and generosity. He reports that, "Out of their most severe trial, their overflowing joy and their extreme poverty welled up in rich generosity. For I testify that they gave as much as they were able, and even beyond their ability. Entirely on their own, they urgently pleaded with us for the privilege of sharing in this service to the saints. And they did not do as we expected, but they gave themselves first to the Lord and then to us in keeping with God's will...But just as you excel in everything – in faith, in speech, in knowledge, in complete earnestness and in your love for us – see that you also excel in this grace of giving." *(Notice in verse 8:1 Paul speaks of the 'grace' God gave the Macedonian church to give so generously and sacrificially; and in verse 8:7 he encourages the Corinthians believers to do the same. Generosity begins with God's grace and love in our hearts for Him, then flows out to others. Your stewardship/ generosity ministry should follow that path.)*

- God repeatedly tells us in Scripture that **He is the owner** of all that is, and that **we are merely stewards,** or managers, of what He has given us. Here are a few passages:
  - Psalm 50:10 – "For every animal of the forest is mine, and the cattle on a thousand hills."
  - Job 41:11 – "Everything under heaven belongs to me."

- Haggai 2:8 – "The silver is mine and the gold is mine, declares the Lord Almighty."
- Psalm 8:6 – "You made him ruler (*not owner*) over the works of your hands; you put everything under his feet."
- Deuteronomy 8:18 – "But remember the Lord your God, for it is he who gives you the ability to produce wealth..."
- Luke 16:11 – 13 - "So, if you have not been trustworthy in handling worldly wealth, who will trust you with true riches? And if you have not been trustworthy with someone else's property, who will give you property of your own? No servant can serve two masters. Either he will hate the one and love the other, or he will be devoted to the one and despise the other. You cannot serve both God and Money."

I have learned from personal experience and in teaching others that it is imperative that a believer grasp these truths on God's ownership and man's stewardship role, and apply them to his/her life *before* they can begin to mature into a biblical steward and generous giver. Any development of a stewardship/generosity ministry MUST establish these foundational truths in the hearts of their people in order to see actual, consistent and long-term growth in their giving of time, talent and treasure toward the resourcing of its vision.

- There are more than 2,300 verses that address some aspect of stewardship. The Bible certainly is our *blueprint* for handling our money, our time, and our talent.

2. Let's look at Christians in North America:
- Our people are experiencing the same bondage to debt that the average non-believer is. For example, the average credit card debt in the U.S. exceeds

$8300. The average church member's credit card debt is no different, especially among younger adults.

- The savings rate hovers around zero to two percent, and sadly, there is little difference between the non-believer and church folks.
- Imagine the blessing, through effective biblical and practical stewardship and generosity education, if the Christians' portion of this debt service could be eliminated and tithed to Kingdom work!
- There are over a million personal bankruptcies in the U.S. each year. How many of those were Christian families?
- What about those home owners who are "upside down" (they owe more than their house is worth), or have been foreclosed or are about to be foreclosed? They certainly need some help in how to better survive in these difficult times.
- Giving to the Lord's work is *down* in proportion to income, even lower than during the Great Depression according to some studies. That certainly affects a church's ability to resource its vision.
- According to Barna Research Online, the proportion of households that tithe their income to their church is around 3%. In another study, they determined that if evangelicals only increased their giving to that ten percent "floor," an additional $150 billion per year would become available annually for Kingdom work.
- Financial stress is a major factor in marital problems and divorce, including Christians.

3. Here is a final and global reason to implement a stewardship/generosity ministry in your church. According to the U.S. Center for World Missions' *Perspectives on the World Christian Movement*, the **greatest global missions'**

need of our churches is "mobilization", or the raising of financial resources for missions. There are thousands of missionaries and candidates (North American and nationals) waiting to go, but there is not enough funding from the churches because they are putting most of their resources into their local ministries. Only four cents of every dollar put into the American church offering plate goes to world, cross-cultural missions[1].

How do these realities affect a church or private school?

1. Limited resources restrict their growth and ministries.
2. Members have less time to volunteer because of their bondage to debt and need to work more hours.
3. Ministry leaders tend to let their budget drive ministry rather than let ministry drive their budget.
4. Morale among staff and leaders suffers because of the struggle for adequate funds. Rather than asking "How will we pay the bills this month?" they would rather ask "What is God calling us to do with all the resources He has blessed us with?"
5. The spiritual growth of members is restricted because of their improper relationship to money, which can be their chief competitor to their love for God. In short, **this is a spiritual issue**, a discipline issue. The core spiritual issue is expressed in these four scriptures: (Suggestion = Distribute these scripture passages with their questions. Have your members ask themselves the questions following each of the listed passages, possibly discussing their answers)
   - Matthew 6:21 – "Where your treasure is your heart will be." (Question = *Is God really my treasure?"*)

---

[1] *Perspectives on the World Christian Movement* course, U.S. Center for World Missions, Pasadena, CA.

- Matthew 6:24 – "You cannot serve God and money." (Question = *"Am I trying to serve both God and money?"*)
- Matthew 13 – the parable of the sower. Concern over things of the world can choke out the Word of God. (Question = *"Are my concerns over finances choking out the Word of God's effect on my life?"*)
- 1 Timothy 6:10 – "For the love of money is a root of all kinds of evil. Some people, eager for money, have wandered from the faith and pierced themselves with many griefs." (Question = *"What in my life is 'piercing' my love for and trust in God's promises? Am I experiencing some grief?"*)

CHAPTER THREE –

HOW?

Please Note = Even though most of these "HOW' ideas are primarily for the church, I hope they will motivate the reader (non-pastor) to eventually volunteer to serve on your church's lay-led stewardship/generosity ministry leadership team (more on this later). In addition to your church, you can also apply what works for a business or school entity. I will also include some specific ideas you can use for a business or school needs.

So, how then can we encourage greater participation in giving to God's global plan? How do we help our people joyfully volunteer their finances, their time and their spiritual gifts toward the church's or organization's vision and mission of glorifying God in reaching the world for Christ? How can we guide them toward being rich toward God and generous like Him?

I think by now you realize the **answer is <u>not</u> more** fund-raising campaigns, or annual stewardship campaigns, or pledge card efforts, although these might be OK occasionally. It is not badgering your folks or pleading with them to meet your budget this year. As stated in the excellent book, "Revolution in Generosity – Transforming Stewards to be Rich toward God", by Wesley K. Willmer, Editor (Moody Press), "The authors in this book are proposing that there is a more God-honoring approach of providing resources – focusing on transforming stewards to be rich toward God." (I was privileged to be one of the 20 authors asked to write a chapter for this book). When you, as a Christian leader, recognize the priority truth of this "slow approach", and embrace it for your church and/or organization, you will begin to experience generosity and "resourcing" from your people that is abundant, consistent, and long-term.

As Randy Alcorn said, "Our approach to money and possessions isn't just important – it's central to our spiritual lives. Our giving is a reflexive response to the grace of God in our lives. It comes out of the transforming work of Christ in us." (Author of *Money, Possessions and Eternity* and *The Treasure Principle*). Another way of putting it is, "It is a discipleship issue". And, isn't that what you want for your people?

In chapters 3-5 I will give you some general guidance and suggestions on "How to bring this about". There is not room enough within the scope of this book to provide all the details on how to successfully implement a stewardship/generosity ministry that brings about this "transformation" toward a culture of generosity. For one, although there are some basic principles applicable to every church, including a business or school environment, each church or organization is unique, and thus their efforts need to be *tailored* to their specific culture, demographics, economics, spiritual maturity, and leadership capabilities. There are many options, methods and resources to choose from in creating your own unique capability.

The other reason I am not trying to include "all you need" to implement your stewardship/generosity ministry is that **I have already tried that!** My original comprehensive Training Kit (titled *"Resourcing Your Vision – A Church Stewardship Ministry Guide")* attempted to provide all you needed as a "do-it-yourself" resource just for churches. It included about 200 hard-copy pages, two CD's and two DVD's containing four hours of video workshop training. What I learned was that it was overwhelming to pastors and church leaders, even after they paid me to conduct a training workshop for their recruited and potential lay-led stewardship/generosity ministry leadership team. I learned that most churches were not able to take my "do-it-yourself" Training

Kit and "make it happen" without a lot of hands-on coaching, equipping and long-term support.

I also found out that they needed someone to hold them accountable to their stated commitment to patiently implement a plan that worked for them, long-term. As a result of my and other's experience, this book is a rewrite of *most* of my original Training Kit to get you motivated and started. But, **you will need some personal help and guidance**, and at the end of this book I'll tell you **where** you can get that help. I also have taken much of the "nuts & bolts" material that was in the original Training Kit, and placed it in our Vision Resourcing Group's website. I show you how to access these FREE resources in the first page of my Appendix One.

In summary, I've talked about the "WHAT?" and the "WHY?" Now let's focus on the "HOW?"

Start with prayer! Here are some items to pray for:
1. Pray that your church leadership team (staff & lay) will be receptive and eventually committed to implementing a stewardship/generosity ministry.
2. Pray that God will raise up the right lay leadership to form your stewardship/generosity ministry team.
3. Pray for your stewardship/generosity ministry team captain, that he/she will have the necessary leadership qualifications and passion for this important ministry.
4. Pray that your congregation will accept and support this ministry.
5. Pray for the help that you are going to need and want.

Forming Your Team

Teamwork divides the task and multiplies the success. Ask God to lead you to the right ones who have the qualifications and the motivation to succeed. He may lead you to individuals you had not even thought of who are the perfect people for this responsibility.

And, **don't use** your "finance committee", if you have one. They usually don't have the skill sets you will need. TAKE YOUR TIME to find the right individuals! Here are some qualities to look for: (these qualities also work for tailored teams managing the stewardship/generosity process for a business or school entity)

1. Well-respected people in your church, but not necessarily well known.
2. They demonstrate an authentic walk with the Lord.
3. Those who have demonstrated their leadership skills and faithfulness.
4. Those who express a passion for this ministry once they have been introduced to it.
5. Those who are givers to their church (Very important!).
6. Those with a willingness to give the necessary time to this effort.

Though the pastor is not actually on the team, he/she is critically important to its success. He/she needs to be the "cheerleader" who encourages and motivates their effort. Again, don't assign the responsibility to one person only to run this ministry. They will overload themselves and prevent others from receiving the blessing of serving in an important and fulfilling ministry. It is also imperative that the church board and the staff (including a business and school) be 100% committed to this stewardship/generosity ministry effort. Spend the time and effort to find them, vet them and bring them on board. **This is where you could use some outside help.** One resource that I'll talk about later allows you to test candidate's strengths, temperament and personality so that all those ending up on your lay-led leadership team are assigned to the right positions that fit their gift-sets. To help them understand what this is all about and gain a passion for this ministry, **they should read this book**.

Your stewardship/generosity ministry leadership team can consist of the positions listed below. The number of positions on your team may differ according to the size of your church (or business

46

or school), but there are **at least three** you should have in order to adequately manage and implement this ministry. The three are *Team Leader, Administration & Communication*, and *Promotion*. Several positions may have to be filled by one individual until you can fill all the positions you want for your team. Be sure to undergird the whole team's efforts with a strong emphasis on PRAYER. As you will see, getting biblical truths and applications on stewardship and generosity into the hearts of your people is a challenge.

NOTE: for a secular business or school entity, there are teaching resources that teach biblical principles without mentioning the bible or specific passages. Some are mentioned in Appendix One.

This is a spiritual battle, and the *Team Leader* needs to lead his/her team continually in prayer over their plans and activities. The following positions are listed by priority to the team, and the number designates the order of *when* to assign the leadership position.

1. *Team Leader* – Provides overall leadership to the ministry. This person will manage, support and coordinate the efforts of each team member. He or she will work with the pastor, staff and board liaison or representative. He or she, along with the pastor, will cast the vision for the effort with the congregation. Some of the qualities that would be desirable in the Team Leader are:
    - A person with good organizational skills.
    - A person who is well respected in the church.
    - A person who can communicate and motivate well.
    - A servant leader who can influence others to reach their potential.

2. *Administration & Communication* – Handles details of their scheduling and activities. It would include database maintenance, communicating to the various ministry leaders affected by the team's activities, registration of folks attending events, ordering materials and collecting

monies for material sales and event registrations. It would also include coordinating prayer support for the team's activities. Look for these qualities:

- A person gifted in handling details.
- A person with a servant's heart who follows through on responsibilities.
- A person who works well with church staff and leaders.
- A person who is respected in the church.
- A person who can communicate prayer requests to the church prayer leaders.

3. *Promotion* – Creates and coordinates all promotions relevant to their team activities, programs and general education events. This will involve the use of strategies such as videos, printed materials, e-mail, website, social media, and vocal. Look for these qualities:

- A person with a bent toward marketing and promotion.
- A person who has a "sales type" personality.
- A person who is creative in producing successful promotion of scheduled events.
- A person who is able to motivate others to action.

The above are the *primary* team positions with *general* job descriptions you will need. As you launch your team and its experience grows, especially with help from experts specializing in this area of ministry, job descriptions will "flesh out" for each position. And you can assign the *following positions* to additional individuals as your activities and events expand for your church.

4. *Worship Services* – Insures that each worship service includes some stewardship/generosity content, or promotion, such as:

- A drama on budgeting, first-time giving or tithing
- A quote from an individual or a biblical passage on the subject

- A testimony from a member on the benefit they received from one of your stewardship/generosity classes or seminars
- A short video on some aspect of the subject.

These are called "stewardship moments", usually conducted during the offering time. This person plans and coordinates with the Senior and/or worship pastor for the inclusion of all promotion and education of stewardship and generosity content during worship services. Often the challenge here is convincing your Senior pastor and/or worship pastor (leader) to cooperate. It can be difficult for them to embrace stewardship or giving as "part" of the worship "experience", even though the bible endorses it. Look for these qualities:

- Ideally, it would be advantageous to have this person also serving on the worship team.
- They are diplomatic and patient.
- They are creative, able to schedule the right content and delivery method for each service.
- They have good communication skills.

5. *Sunday School or Christian Education Teaching* – If you have a formal Sunday School or Christian Education program that includes adults, youth, and children, this team leader plans, schedules, and coordinates the teaching of stewardship/generosity in all your classes, working closely with assigned pastors, lay leaders, and teachers. This person provides selected teaching content and ensures that each class is provided trained and qualified teachers when teaching the content. Look for these qualities:

- A person who knows the organizational structure and the people involved in your Sunday School ministry and/or Christian education program.
- A person with strong organizational gifts.
- A person who has a servant's heart, seeking to assist and empower your Christian education leaders and

teachers in bringing stewardship education to their groups.

6. *Small Group Ministry* – Works closely with your Small Group pastor or lay leader in promoting and scheduling the inclusion of stewardship/generosity material and studies designed for small groups. This team leader coordinates the small group teaching schedule with the general agenda and schedule of the Stewardship/Generosity leadership team as well as the church master calendar. Look for these qualities:

- Has experience participating in and leading a small group.
- Has organizational skill.
- Has communication and diplomatic talent.
- Has a servant-leadership heart.

7. *Seminars* - Schedules, promotes and coordinates all stewardship/generosity seminars, whether live or video. Works with other team leaders and church staff in scheduling, promoting and conducting selected seminars. Look for these qualities:

- Good at marketing and promotion.
- Well organized.
- Diplomatic and patient.
- Has a servant-leadership heart.

8. *Estate and Gift Planning* – Understands the terminology, process, and technical aspects of estate and gift planning. Ensures that church attendees and members are motivated and instructed in the "why" and "how" of estate and planned giving through seminars and available personal consultations. Works with the team, the seminar leader and church staff in providing and promoting seminars on this topic. Locates, recruits and vets licensed professionals to conduct the seminars and provides for personal follow-up consultations. Look for these qualities:

- Has experience in the financial and/or legal services profession.
- Has promotional skill.
- Has communication skill.
- Has a servant-leadership heart.

9. ***Counselor Team*** - Develops a trained team of available counselors who can *personally* counsel and mentor individuals and couples seeking help with their money management and debt reduction. This person most likely would be a trained counselor who utilized training received from ministries like *Vision Resourcing Group, Crown, and Good $ense Ministry.* Look for these qualities:
   - Has been trained as a personal counselor in budgeting and money management.
   - Is patient and compassionate.
   - Can lead by example in their own personal finances.
   - Is able to commit the time necessary to counsel and lead this sub-team of counselors.

10. ***Special Events and Campaigns*** - Coordinates all the details of running a stewardship and generosity education special event or campaign to raise funds for selected projects. This job could be combined with Seminars. Chances are this person will work with a professional consultant who specializes in capital campaigns or fund-raising events. It depends on the purpose and size of the campaign or event. Look for these qualities:
   - Someone who is very organized and can attend to details.
   - Someone who works well with other team members and church staff.
   - Someone who can motivate other leaders in the church.

11. ***Church Board Liaison or Representative*** – This person communicates between the church board and the stewardship/generosity leadership team in order to ensure

that both groups of leaders are on the same page and coordinating their respective activities. Although this person doesn't do any of the work, he/she is important for communication and representation. It would be good to recruit a board member who has participated in some stewardship and generosity ministry teaching. This will help them understand what the team does and needs.

12. *Pastoral Staff Representative* - This person communicates between the church staff and the stewardship/generosity leadership team in order to ensure that both groups of leaders are on the same page and coordinating their respective activities. Although this person doesn't do any of the work, he/she is important for communication and representation. It would be good to recruit a staff member who has participated in some stewardship and generosity ministry teaching. This will help them understand what the team does and needs.

The above list represents all the possible positions on the stewardship/generosity ministry leadership team, even though you may never need them all, or be able to grow to that size. Certainly all of your leaders need to be willing to serve, at a minimum, for a year, as this is a long-term process. They all need to demonstrate a good and consistent Christian walk with the Lord and have a strong interest in this particular ministry. And, you need to make sure they are carefully screened and tested to make sure they fit their particular assigned position. As with any church ministry, or any organization for that matter, quality leadership is essential for success. Finally, don't hesitate to seek some professional help in order to properly screen and test them.

On the following page is a blank Church Stewardship/Generosity Ministry Leadership Team *organizational chart*. Use it to begin the process of recruiting candidates God leads you to as you form your team. Start slow, and don't feel that you have to fill in all the positions at the beginning. The names you pencil down start out as only "candidates", and no decision should be made until they have been vetted, trained and have committed to their particular position and job description. This will take months to get the right individuals, but it is well worth the effort.

Church Stewardship/Generosity Ministry Leadership Team (candidates)

Team Leader _____
Phone = _____
E-mail _____

Administration &
*Communication*_____
Phone = _____
E-mail _____

Promotion _____
Phone = _____
E-mail _____

Worship Services _____
Phone = _____
E-mail _____

Sunday School or Christian Education Teaching
_____
Phone = _____
E-mail _____

*Small Group Ministry*_____
Phone = _____
E-mail _____

Seminars _____
Phone = _____
E-mail _____

Estate and Gift Planning _____

Phone = _____

E-mail _____

Counselor Team _____

Phone = _____

E-mail _____

Special Events and Campaigns

_____

Phone = _____

E-mail _____

Church Board Liaison or
*Representative*_____

Phone = _____

E-mail _____

Pastoral Staff Representative

_____

Phone = _____

E-mail _____

Introducing your stewardship/ generosity ministry to your people

Once you have formed and trained your initial stewardship/ generosity leadership team, it is time to start the process of introducing this ministry and your newly formed leadership team to your congregation. You will need to motivate them to cooperate in completing the *Stewardship/Generosity Questionnaire*. The *Questionnaire* is foundational for completing the *Organizational Stewardship/Generosity Survey,* which is foundational for establishing your long-term agenda. Because you may encounter some resistance to the very personal questions, here are some suggested items to communicate:

1. Share the "big picture" that the leadership is committed to educating them in the "whole counsel" of God's word. Stewardship and generosity are a vital part of this process.

2. Evidence indicates that there is a strong felt-need for help in becoming better managers of our money and time, especially during these challenging economic times.

3. The Bible and Jesus have a lot to say about finances and possessions.

4. The leadership is committed to your spiritual growth in the Lord. This includes how well you are doing in the areas of stewardship and generosity, which are a vital part of discipleship.

5. Our newly formed stewardship/generosity ministry leadership team will be providing educational and training opportunities and integrating their agenda with our master calendar and ministry activities.

6. In order for them to better help and equip you for this growth, they need to know your **honest** and current spiritual health. This includes your **honest** financial and giving status.

7. The results from this **anonymous** *Stewardship/Generosity Questionnaire* will greatly help them in designing a stewardship and generosity educational agenda that works for you.

8. We really need your **candid** and **anonymous** response. **DON'T WRITE YOUR NAME** on the questionnaire! THANK YOU FOR YOU HELP so we can HELP YOU!

Here is a **sample** *Stewardship/Generosity Questionnaire* (which can be tailored to your specific needs):

Stewardship/Generosity Questionnaire

We would appreciate your **candid** and **anonymous** response. In order to serve you better in the area of stewardship and generosity education, and carry out our church's vision and global mission, we need your input and information. **DO NOT WRITE YOUR NAME** on the questionnaire. **It is anonymous**. Give totals as a family unit, not individual family members. Your candid answers will help us in designing an effective stewardship and generosity teaching agenda. Thank you so much!

Signed "Your Stewardship/Generosity Ministry Leadership Team."

1. How long has your family been attending church?
   1-5 yrs_____ 6-10 yrs_____ Over 10 yrs _____
2. How many total years have your family members known the Lord Jesus Christ as their personal Savior?_____ Describe the quality of their walk with the Lord _____
   _____
   _____
   _____
3. Does your family know their spiritual gift(s)?
   Yes _____ No _____
4. Is your family currently giving of their time and talent in a church ministry? Yes___ No _____
5. What is your average *gross* family *annual* income?
   $25,000 to $49,999 _____ $50,000 to $74,999 _____
   $75,000 to $99,999 _____ More than $100,000_____
6. Do you have a current *written* budget that you follow daily?
   Yes _____ No _____
7. On average, are you spending more than your income each month? Yes _____ No _____
8. What is the current balance of your credit card debt? Zero ____ $1000 to $5000 ____ More____
9. What *percentage* of your gross family *annual* income do you currently give to the church?
   1-3% _____ 3-4% _____ 4-5% _____ 5-6% _____
   6-7%____ 7-8% _____ 8-9% _____ More ____

10. What *percentage* of your *gross* family *annual* income do you currently give to other ministries? _____What is the total *percentage* given to church & ministry? _____
11. Do you have a current written will or living trust? Yes _____ No _____
12. If you have a current written will or living trust, does it include a charitable bequest for the Lord's work? Yes _____ No _____
13. Is our church included? Yes _____ No _____
14. Would you be interested in receiving training in biblical money management, stewardship principles and estate planning? Yes _____ No _____
15. What specific subjects or themes do you want to learn about? _____
_____
16. Do you have any special needs, observations or comments?
_____
_____
_____

Note: If you have the technical capability to put the *Stewardship/ Generosity Questionnaire* on your website, you could have your people complete them electronically over the Internet. Once you have a good sample of completed *Questionnaires*, they will supply you with much of the information you will need in order to complete your *Organizational Stewardship/Generosity Survey*. The evaluation of the results of this survey will help prepare you in designing your activity agenda. After you tabulate the answers from the *Stewardship/Generosity Questionnaires,* use the answers to complete the *Organizational Stewardship/Generosity Survey* along with personal interviews with pastoral and/or your administrative staff, especially your finance chairperson and/or bookkeeper. Here is a **sample** *Organizational Stewardship/ Generosity Survey:*

Organizational Stewardship/Generosity Survey

(I am giving you a **sample** here with *hypothetical* answers to show you the kind of information you are looking for to help prepare your strategy and agenda; this happens to be a church)

CHURCH ___*First Church*__ PHONE _____*(601) 456-78*___

ADDRESS _____*435 East Main St*_____

CITY _____*Coastal Town*_____ ST __*CA*___ ZIP __*90334*__

PASTOR ____*John Knox*_____

AVERAGE ATTENDANCE _*235*__

1. Describe the demographics of your church, i.e., age & ethnic mix, professional, "blue collar," single versus married, etc. *ave. age = 35; anglo and Hispanic; blue collar; mostly couples*____
2. Describe your *perception* of the spiritual condition of your members and attendees. ____*most are younger Christians, just learning the basics on how to walk with the Lord*____
3. Does your church teach spiritual gifts? _____*no*_____
4. How well do your people offer their time and talent to the ministry of the church? _____*could be better; about 15% do most of the work*_____
5. Is your church receiving adequate finances? Are you meeting your budget requirements? *we are barely keeping our heads above water each year with no room for expansion*___
6. What was your church's *average* income per year the past three years? _*about $500,000*____
7. What is your Sunday morning attendance percentage growth per year compared to giving income percentage growth, if any, the past five years? _*about even*___
8. What money did your church receive the past five years from bequests? _____*none*__

9. How do you "raise money" for your church? Events? Preaching? Other? __*Weekly offering during worship services and two sermons a year*__

10. If the church had sufficient finances, what would be its priority goals for ministry? __*pay off debt of $100,000; have worship pastor go full-time; replace carpet in children's Sunday school class*__

11. What percentage of the church budget is allocated for missions? ___*10%*___

12. How are mission funds raised? It is part of our church budget ___ Faith promises, over and above regular giving ___*x*___ Specific designation _____Other_____

13. The individual average annual *gross income* of our family units is _____*$60,000*_____

14. What is the average percent of gross family income that your people *say* they are giving to the church? ___*5*___
To other ministries? ___*2*___ Total? ___*7*___

15. What percent of their annual *gross income,* on average, are they <u>actually</u> giving to the church? _____*3*_____

16. What is the *potential* giving of your people if they were to tithe the *full ten percent* of their gross income to the church? _____*$1,200,000*_____ (Multiply the number of households, or giving "units," by their *average* gross family income by ten percent. You determine the *average* gross family income from the replies you receive off the questionnaires you distributed.)

17. What percentage of your people have a written will or living trust? ___*35%*___

18. What percentage of those who *have a will or trust* have included a charitable bequest for the Lord's work, including your church? _*5%*_ What percent would like to? *65%*_____

19. What percentage of your people have a written budget that they are following daily? *7%*_

20. What percentage of your people are spending, on average, *more* than they make each month? _____*20%*_____

21. What is the average amount of credit debt (other than house mortgage) that your people are carrying each month? ___ *$8200* ___

22. What stewardship education has been provided by the church for your people? ___ *just started Crown Financial Ministry class* __

23. What specific training in stewardship have your people requested? __ *budgeting class and how to get out of debt* __

24. How well do you think your people are managing their personal finances? __ *about as good as the average American* ___

25. Do you think they would benefit from some practical and biblical training in the area of financial management and estate planning? Yes _x_ No ___ Explain. ___ *our young couples need budget and debt reduction training and our older folks need to get their estate plans in order* ___

26. In what priority areas of stewardship education and development do you as a church most feel the need for help and training? *starting a stewardship ministry* __

27. Any other observations or comments? ___ *we want to start educating our people in stewardship without giving them the impression that we just want their money* _

Here is a *blank* Church Stewardship Survey you can edit for your church purposes:

Organizational Stewardship/Generosity Survey

CHURCH _____

PHONE _____

ADDRESS _____

CITY _____ ST _____ ZIP _____

PASTOR _____

AVERAGE ATTENDANCE _____

1. Describe the demographics of your church, i.e. age & ethnic mix, professional, "blue collar", single verses married, etc. _____

   _____

2. Describe your *perception* of the spiritual condition of your members and attendees. _____

   _____

3. Does your church teach spiritual gifts? _____

4. How well do your people offer their time and talent to the ministry of the church? _____

5. Is your church receiving adequate finances? Are you meeting your budget requirements? _____

6. What was your church's *average* income per year the past three years? _____

7. What is your Sunday morning attendance percentage growth per year compared to giving income percentage growth, if any, the past five years? _____

8. What money did your church receive the past five years from bequests? _____

9. How do you "raise money" for your church? Events? Preaching? Other? _____

   _____

   If the church had sufficient finances, what would be its priority goals for ministry? _____

   _____

10. What percentage of the church budget is allocated for missions? _____

11. How are mission funds raised? It is part of our church budget ___ Faith promises, over and above regular giving ___ Specific designation ___ Other _____

12. The individual average annual *gross income* of our people is _____

13. What is the average percent of gross family income that your people *say* they are giving to the church? _____ To other ministries? _____ Total? _____

14. What percent of their annual *gross income,* on average, are they <u>actually</u> giving to the church? _____

15. What is the *potential* giving of your people if they were to tithe the *full ten percent* of their gross income to the church? _____ (Multiply the number of households, or giving "units", by their *average* gross family income by ten percent. You determine the *average* gross family income from the replies you receive off the questionnaires you distributed.)

16. What percentage of your people have a written will or living trust? _____

17. What percentage of those who *have a will or trust* have included a charitable bequest for the Lord's work, including your church? _____ What percent would like to? _____

18. What percentage of your people have a written budget that they are following daily? _____

19. What percentage of your people are spending, on average, *more* than they make each month? _____

20. What is the average amount of credit debt (other than house mortgage) that your people are carrying each month? _____
_____

21. What stewardship education has been provided by the church for your people? _____
_____

22. What specific training in stewardship have your people requested?_____
_____

23. How well do you think your people are managing their personal finances?_____

_____

24. Do you think they would benefit from some practical and biblical training in the area of financial management and estate planning? Yes___No___Explain _____

_____

25. In what priority areas of stewardship education and development do you as a church most feel the need for help and training? _____

26. Any other observations or comments? _____

_____

_____

_____

_____

GETTING STARTED

Where do you start? That depends on the results from your *Stewardship/Generosity Questionnaires* and your *Organizational Stewardship/Generosity Survey*. It also depends on your research of available resources, the readiness of your new stewardship/ generosity ministry leadership team, your other organizational ministry priorities and master calendar, and available staff and lay leadership to provide logistical and financial support. If you bring in professional help to consult, equip and support your efforts, this ministry will grow much faster with better results. But, start slow, be realistic, and don't try to do too much at first.

The information gleaned from the *Questionnaires* and *Survey* will help you pick the activities and events that seem most important to your people and that you have the capability to implement. It will take time for your stewardship/generosity leadership team members and organization staff, who may end up doing some of the teaching, to gain experience and capability in this new ministry. But, in the long run, the payoff is well worth it. As your people experience transformation in becoming rich towards God, they will become more generous as He is generous. And you will begin to see an increase in giving of their time, talent and treasure without you having to conduct high-pressure campaigns and efforts to raise the budget.

To summarize, you learned what your stewardship/generosity leader team should look like and how to form it. I showed you how to introduce a stewardship ministry to your people and how to survey them in order to gain insight into their stewardship & generosity "health." Having worked with churches of different sizes and persuasions, I know how difficult it is to "choose the right path." That is why it would be very helpful if you took advantage of some professional help. But, to get you started let's talk about developing and activating your agenda once your leadership team is in place and trained.

> *"I will instruct you and teach you in the*
> *way you should go; I will guide you with my eye."*
> *Psalm 32:8 (NKJ)*

AGENDA

Developing and Activating Your Agenda

Now that you have tabulated the results of the *Stewardship/Generosity Questionnaires*, completed and evaluated the results of the *Organizational Stewardship/Generosity Survey*, and calculated *Your Church's or Ministry's Giving Potential*, you can begin to design and schedule your *Stewardship/Generosity Ministry* activities and themes to teach. The evaluation of all this information will guide you as you design and schedule your agenda. This will vary with each church or organization. What proved to be the strongest felt-need of your people, by age group? Where are they the weakest? Your stewardship/generosity leadership team, along with counsel from your pastoral or organizational staff, will need to decide which activities are the most important at the start. Don't try to do everything at once. Commit to what your current leadership resources can handle, start slowly, and gradually add activities over time. Remember, **it will take time** to bring your people to their full stewardship and generous maturity.

To guide you as you begin this process of developing your agenda, here are some *characteristics* of an effective stewardship/generosity *education* ministry:

- It is rooted in sound *biblical thinking*. Scripture undergirds all of your chosen events, teaching activities and produced copy for worship folders, website etc.
- It is *age-group specific* and *culturally appropriate*. It is sensitive to each age-group being addressed as well as their specific culture. An example of a "specific" group is "military couples with small children in your Hispanic congregation". You would structure your teaching material and scheduling differently then with your "Anglo senior adults".
- It addresses *real life issues* and meets people at their point of need. Offer classes and/or personal counseling on subjects they have expressed in your *stewardship/generosity questionnaire,* such as "How to get out of debt", "Personal budgeting", "Why God wants you to give" etc.
- It focuses on *developing Christian values* and life principles. Include topics like "honesty", "work", "God owns it all" etc.
- It encompasses a *total-life view* of stewardship and generosity. You want to cover more than just *giving, the tithe,* or the *budget.* Include their use of *time* and *talent.*
- It is done *with excellence*. This teaching and counseling is so important to their spiritual health that you want to insist on every activity, event and communication being done to the best of your ability in quality and effectiveness.
- It should be *interesting* and highly *visual*. Use the most effective and state-of-the-art methods and tools to

communicate your messages. Because your people are suffering from information overload, you need to *compete* with all of the rest of communications they are receiving daily by making yours the best.

- It is sustained and *ongoing*. It recognizes that it takes time to transform believers into mature stewards and generous givers. To succeed in their hearts requires repetition, repetition, repetition!

THEMES

Some **KEY QUESTIONS** to answer as you develop your agenda are: "What should you teach?" "What are the various themes to include?" "Which ones are priority?" Here is a *basic overview*, with selected Scriptures of stewardship and generosity *themes* to study and teach, listed in order by priority:

- **God's part** – He owns everything we possess, including our bodies, our time, our gold and silver, and our talent. Getting your people to understand and fully accept this basic truth is *critical* to guiding them to mature stewardship and generosity. It takes time and repetition for this truth to become a part of their inner being, starting with you the organization leadership team. You will want to lead by example.
  - God owns it all—Psalm 50:10; 24:1; Haggai 2:8; 1 Chronicles 29:11-12; Leviticus 25:23
  - God is Lord of all—Genesis 1:1; Job 42:2; Psalm 135:6; Acts 17:26; Colossians 2:15
  - He is the provider of all—Psalm 16:5-6; Matthew 6:25-32; Ephesians 1:3; Philippians 4:19
- **Man's part** – We have a vital part, as "managers" (stewards) of all that God has given us. This truth also needs to be "repeated' into the hearts and minds of your people.
  - We are stewards—Genesis 1:26; Psalm 8:4-6; Leviticus 25:23; Hebrews 11:13

- We are to be faithful—1 Corinthians 4:2; Luke 16:10-12; "Small things are small things, but faithfulness with a small thing is a big thing" (Hudson Taylor); Matthew 25:23
- We are held accountable—Luke 12:48; Romans 14:12; 2 Corinthians 5:10

- **Managing our time and talent** – They are God-given. Use them for His pleasure, glory, and to benefit the body of Christ.
  - God created our time and place on earth—Acts 17:26; Luke 12:19-20
  - God created our talent and spiritual gifts—Ephesians 2:10; 1 Peter 4:10-11; 1 Corinthians 12:1-11; Romans 12:6-8
  - Don't waste time--- Ephesians 5:15-17; Psalm 90:12; Ecclesiastes 3:1
  - Work with all your heart for the Lord—Colossians 3:23-24
  - Don't presume on your future—James 4:13-15
  - Be diligent in all that you do—Proverbs 22:29; 27:23
  - Don't forget to rest—Exodus 20:9-10

- **Managing our money** – Provide biblical and practical teaching to help your people.
  - Don't love money—1 Timothy 6:10; Ecclesiastes 5:10
  - Be content with what you have—1 Timothy 6:6-8; Philippians 4:11-13; Hebrews 13:5
  - Don't live beyond your means—Proverbs 21:17
  - Be sure to save and invest—Proverbs 21:5, 20; 30:24-25; Genesis 41:34-36
  - Don't cosign notes—Proverbs 17:18; 22:26-27
  - Don't over-use credit cards—Proverbs 27:12
  - Set financial goals—Proverbs 16:9 LB; 24:2-4
  - Have an up-to-date estate plan—2 Kings 20:1

- Establish and work a budget—Proverbs 27:23-24
- Be willing to seek financial counsel—Proverbs 12:15
- Avoid debt—Romans 13:8; Proverbs 22:7
- Pay your debts—Psalm 37:21; Proverbs 3:27-28

- **Giving our money, time and talent** – If we desire to become like Jesus, we will let His Spirit within us express His generosity through us.
  - In Lesson Ten of my Appendix One, I have given you a simple outline on "Why Should We Give?". You can use it for a sermon or teaching outline.
  - More blessed to give—Acts 20:35; Luke 6:38. One author puts it this way, "Generosity is a gateway into intimacy with God."
  - Let love motivate your giving—1 Corinthians 13:3
  - Give cheerfully—2 Corinthians 9:7; 8:2-3; Acts 4:32-36
  - Give systematically—1 Corinthians 16:2
  - Give proportionately—2 Corinthians 8:12-13
  - Give sacrificially—Hebrews 13:16
  - Give first to God before yourself—Proverbs 3:9
  - Give ten percent—Malachi 3:10; 2 Corinthians 9:6
  - "You can give without loving, but you cannot love without giving."

- **Training our children** – Teach them while they are young, and you will prepare them for a life of financial freedom, intimacy with God, and the joy of generosity. Proverbs 22:6; Deuteronomy 6:6-7;11:18-19; Ephesians 6:4

- **Taxes** – Don't cheat, but it's OK to minimize taxes with counsel and wise management. Matthew 22:17-21; Romans 13:1-7

- **Estate and gift planning** – It is important to teach your people to properly establish their estate plans which can, in some cases, lead to significant deferred gifts. We'll give

you some good ideas on how to do this later in the book. 2
Kings 20:1

*To successfully penetrate the hearts of your people, you must
repeatedly teach the stewardship themes from every ministry
platform ("faucet") you can.*

**Here is my "formula" for a successful
stewardship/generosity ministry":**

**Long-term stewardship & generosity education and
activities**
       + a shared ministry vision
       + a well-designed ministry plan
       + passionate prayer
       + passionate leadership

**= growing and mature followers of Jesus Christ who
provide abundant resources to carry out the global
ministry vision of your church or organization.**

OK, what are some **specific venues or "platforms"** you can use to
educate and train your people to become better stewards and
generous givers? As mentioned earlier, your people are suffering
from *"information overload"*, plus the persistent influence of
society's worldview. They will need to be continuously "exposed"
to God's worldview and instruction in these areas. To use the
analogy mentioned before, your church or organization has a
"water system" of multiple ministries, departments and
"platforms" from which your people "drink" from to receive God's
truths and guidance. Examples of these "faucets" are the church
pulpit, Christian education class, new member's class, worship
folders, newsletter, website, seminars, pre-marriage counseling,
etc.

As you consider specific activities and events that you can include in your agenda, it is important to remember that you will want to pick only the ones that fit your capability or interest at a given time. You may only want to offer two activities for the first year, such as a small group financial Bible study and four sermons. As you gain experience, capability and confidence, you may end up doing most of them, utilizing the "services" of a full stewardship/ generosity leadership team. And, of course, getting some outside help and training can speed up the process and your capability. See the following list.

POSSIBLE ACTIVITIES AND EVENTS
(Not all will apply to a business or school)

Preaching

Preaching must be a consistent part of your church stewardship and generosity education process. Some pastors will pick a month each year to preach a series on biblical stewardship. Four or five sermons on the subject can provide good motivation and basic education on stewardship and generosity principles. By itself, it doesn't "cut" that deep, but it gets the message out to almost everybody, and it is important because it shows the people where your pastor is on the subject and demonstrates his/her faithfulness to teach the whole counsel of God's Word. At the same time, be sure to include other avenues of teaching around the time of stewardship sermons to complement and reinforce the messages. Also, remind your pastor that his/her stewardship sermons should **not** only be on "giving." I have provided a few sample sermon outlines and sources of messages on the topic in Appendix One with others on our website.

Worship

Worship services themselves provide an important opportunity to teach stewardship and generosity besides just through preaching. What about the offering opportunity? Instead of just asking the ushers to come forward and then pray, why not take one or two minutes *before* the offering to have a *"stewardship moment"*? These moments can include the following options:

1. A brief testimony given by someone in your church who has benefited from stewardship or giving growth, such as tithing or getting out of credit card debt. Be sure to check the testimony for brevity and preparation! Test them first to make sure they adhere to your worship time-constraints. Have the person testify how God led and blessed him/her spiritually in their stewardship decision. A good way of controlling the quality and time generated is to video tape these people giving their testimony, allowing you to edit and/or re-tape them.

2. Have someone from your worship team or stewardship/ generosity ministry leadership team read a *verse* or *quote* some aspect of stewardship and generosity. I have provided some verses and quotes in Appendix One, and more on our website, to get you started.

3. If your church does drama in your worship services, include ones on stewardship and generosity, especially if you want to reinforce a sermon series on the subject.

4. Be sure to include *ministry reports* of what God is doing in some ministry of the church or missions, indicating that their giving helped make it possible. This serves as a reminder and encouragement to your congregation.

Keep these moments positive, to complement the other activities of stewardship education. One of your stewardship/generosity leadership team will need to be assigned the responsibility of coordinating these activities with your church worship team.

All-Church Tithing Sunday

Think of these two options as an "eye opener" and challenge to your congregation.

- *Option one* = Have everyone *in advance* bring a full 10% of their <u>average</u> monthly income as an offering on a *designated* Sunday.
- *Option two* = Have everyone bring a card, on a *designated* Sunday, stating what the full 10% of their <u>average</u> monthly income would be if they actually gave the full tithe. Be sure to emphasize that they should NOT indicate their name, but keep the information anonymous.
- Tally this information, and report the totals back to the congregation. People will be amazed, shocked, and challenged. They will discover that if they faithfully gave 10% of their income, as a congregation, to the Lord's work through their local church that they could expand the church budget two to four times for missions, staff, new ministries and regular operations.

Sunday School and Christian Education Classes

Sunday School and Christian Education Classes for your adults and youth may be an important area of your Sunday education effort. I've included a few lesson outlines for your use in appendix one, plus more on our website. For your youth and children, a great option is to use these studies to teach their parents so that they can then teach their children. Can you imagine what our churches would be like if we all would have been taught these truths at an early age? In Appendix Two, on our list of "other ministry resources" in the back of this book, some offer specific studies for youth and children.

Small Groups

In a small group, people can be loved, encouraged and held accountable. This loving accountability motivates the participants to apply what they learn. One of the greatest benefits of a small group approach is the opportunity to build close personal relation-ships. Using a small group setting for stewardship education is one of the most effective methods in students' lives. Be sure to include a small group component in your stewardship/ generosity ministry.

Several of the organizations listed in Appendix Two provide studies for small groups.

One on One

There should be a place in your stewardship/generosity ministry for personal or one on one counsel. Some of your people will need that personal help and encouragement, along with accountability, that a group setting does not provide. Often the seminar or class will stimulate them to want to take action, but they will need some personal guidance, particularly in the area of budgeting and debt reduction. This means that you will want to form a small group of trained budget counselors who can be available to individually help these people. These counselors can be professionally trained financial planners, or folks who have led several small group financial bible studies available from several ministries. Some of these ministries also offer small group leadership training for individuals interested in this ministry. This is a very time-intensive ministry, and interested counselor candidates need to be reminded of the necessary time commitment they will have to make before signing up.

Written Materials

Remembering that people learn in different ways and that they need that repetition of content, even in small bits, be sure to include written materials. Here are some suggestions:

- *Organization Newsletter*—Include a section or column in your organization newsletter, hard copy or on your website, on the subject of stewardship and generosity. This can be monthly, or as often as one is published. Your Communication leader is responsible for getting copy to your newsletter on a regular basis. They can draw from some of the copy and listed websites provided in this book's appendices and our website. You can also include people's written testimony about their pilgrimage with regard to money. This could be a real encouragement to others reading their account. A possible title for this column is "T3," which stands for *"time, talent & treasure."* Here is a suggested *intro* to your "T3" column:

"Where is your heart? If you are not sure, look for your 'treasure'. Jesus said in Matthew 6:21, 'For where your treasure is, there your heart will be also.' If you want to have a heart for His kingdom, give of yourself to it, and your heart will follow. This is the introduction to our new 'T3' column in (name your newsletter here). In determining where your heart is, ask yourself how you are doing with your three 'T's'. In this column we will be sharing encouragement and ideas to help all of us become better stewards and givers of our time, talent and our treasure. Our 'T3' stewardship/generosity ministry at (your church or school name) is committed to helping all of us become the faithful stewards and givers God wants us to be."

- *Church or School Library*—There are many excellent books, booklets, audiocassettes and DVD's on the subject of stewardship and generosity, and these can be supplied to your church or school library. Obviously you will want to publicize their availability to your people. You can find them at your neighborhood Christian book store and/or through the websites listed in Appendix Two or ones you find on your own.

- *Church Worship Folder*—Along with any announcements on stewardship and generosity events and activities, this is a good place to include quotes, verses and mini-articles on some aspect of the subjects. Again, this is a simple way to keep the subject in front of your people. Some samples are provided in Appendix One and on our website.

- *Articles*—You may want to occasionally distribute to your people copies of good articles on some aspect of stewardship and generosity. A few are provided in Appendix One and our website.

- *Bulletin Boards*—Develop displays and provide a "people friendly" bulletin board located strategically in the organization facility. Change the material frequently. Provide informational handouts.

- *Send Thank-you Letters* to individuals who have been faithful in their giving. Also, mail (and/or e-mail) general letters to your donors, thanking them for their support and reminding them of how their giving has helped produce the indicated ministry results.

New Church Member Classes

Your Church New Member Class is the opportunity to share the vision and mission of your church. And it is a wonderful opportunity to share your heart for stewardship and generosity. Use this class to "start them right" toward not only understanding the basics of stewardship and generosity, but of recognizing their responsibility and privilege of supporting the mission of the church.

Pre-Marital Counseling

This is also a wonderful opportunity to assist a couple planning on getting married. I wish I had been given good stewardship and generosity instruction before getting married! Encourage them to take a small group Bible study class on biblical finances. Have them sit through one of your Sunday school stewardship/generosity classes on budgeting and debt reduction. This can save them a lot of grief later on, since a major cause of marital stress and distress is financial mismanagement.

Retreats

As I have stressed, *repetition* is important for learning. And retreats are another good "exposure" of stewardship/generosity principles for your people. Most adult retreats have workshops or breakout sessions as part of their agenda. Don't forget to occasionally include a session on some aspect of stewardship and generosity.

Seminars

Seminars are an exceptionally good source for stewardship and generosity education. A lot of information can be packed into a single two to six hour seminar. You will want one of your Team members to give leadership to coordinating, promoting and conducting the seminars. The actual teaching of the seminar may be a video or live presentation by trained professionals. I provide some practical ideas on how to promote, conduct and follow-up seminars later in Chapter Four.

Miscellaneous

- **Say Thanks!** You are competing with other philanthropic institutions that are saying thanks. Send out thank-you letters. Print thank-you comments on giving reports, ministry up-dates and vision casting. Make thank-you phone calls to your *consistent* givers, not just your "big ones." Divide these calls among staff and key leaders.
- **Collect and Share Ministry Stories.** Collect stories from your church or school ministry leaders about the difference that giving from your donors is making locally and beyond. Get stories from missionaries and organizations you support as a ministry. Print these in your newsletter, or use videos to share them at worship services or other functions. They put a "face" on the facts and figures of what God is doing through the giving of your people.
- **Hold a Ministry or Mission Fair.** Annually have every ministry represented with displays in a single place to share their focus, service and stories. This will excite members who often don't realize the full scope of the ministries their church supports. It also gives the different leaders of these ministries an opportunity to recruit involvement from church members and attendees.
- **Fund Your Stewardship/Generosity Ministry.** It costs money to implement a stewardship/generosity ministry,

year after year. Be sure to include a line-item on your budget to cover this important expense.

- **Consider Establishing an Endowment Fund.** A good one to start with is a Missions Endowment Fund where you invite people to make major gifts into the fund that disperses the annual earnings to designated missions or ministries. Consult a professional who can assist you in legally setting up the fund. Many donors like the idea of giving to an endowment fund where their money can "work" annually for their ministry of interest. It will not diminish their regular giving to church operations.
- **Offering Envelopes.** If you are not doing so already, provide offering envelopes to members and friends to encourage regular giving. They also serve as a reminder to give during those times when they may be on vacation or away on a given Sunday.
- **Electronic Transfers.** More and more people today are comfortable using electronic transfers for regular payments, such as insurance premiums, and they sometimes like the convenience of giving this way. This also helps in keeping them faithful in their giving. Consider setting up your receipting system to accommodate these people. You might also consider arranging your web page, if you have one, to allow for this type of giving. Here are a couple of websites that provide for both offering envelopes and electronic transfer: www.cathedralstewardship.com and www.MyChurchDonations.com.
- **Home Visits.** Organize visits or focus groups in the homes of church members or school families, not to secure commitments but to get better acquainted. You will want to find out how they are doing, what their ministry passion is, and if they have any suggestions for leaders regarding the operation of the church or school and its ministries. Ask what felt needs they might have, and ask for prayer requests. It is also a good time to thank them personally for their commitment and support.

- **Conduct a Time and Talent Survey.** Annually promote and carry out a broad-based survey that allows members and friends to indicate ways in which they want to invest their time, talent and energy in the coming months. Give them a list of ministry needs in the church or school. This will remind them of the responsibility and blessing of getting involved and giving of themselves.
- **Conduct a Spiritual Gifts Seminar.** Your people need to know what their spiritual gifts are. These are divine gifts just as financial resources are divine gifts, and learning to manage these gifts is the life-long challenge of deepening ones understanding of discipleship and Christian living. It will help them better give of their "talent."
- **Have a Brokerage Account.** It is relatively easy for a church or school to open an account with a stockbroker for the purpose of receiving gifts of securities. Gifts of appreciated stock are not only valuable to the church or school, but they also have significant tax advantages for the contributor. Clear policy guidelines should be in place regarding the processing, holding, or sale of such stock. Professional counsel regarding these transfers is essential.
- **Include Your Youth and Children in Your Stewardship/Generosity Ministry.** Not only teach youth and children through all of the ministry "faucets" available at your church or school, but also teach their parents to teach them as well. Challenge them to tithe. Provide offering envelopes. Place your mature youth on some of your committees in order to gain from their perspective and to encourage them to have a sense of ownership of what God is doing through their church and school. Include them in ushering teams and skits during worship hours. And include them in any capital campaign.

Promoting Your Stewardship/Generosity Ministry

This is done regularly as you "activate" the different parts of the ministry. As you promote a seminar, the next small group financial

Bible study, or a special budgeting class, your people will start accepting this effort as part of their activities and discipleship growth. Your stewardship/generosity ministry leadership team is responsible for coordinating the communication of stewardship ministry activities to your people via the newsletter, worship folders, verbal, e-mail, website, etc. Depending on the communication resources and capability of your organization, you will be able to keep the stewardship "message" in front of your people year after year. Look for creative ways to repeatedly remind your people of this important aspect of their Christian walk.

Occasionally tie your stewardship promotion and ministry needs to your vision and mission. You will want a balance between "generic" stewardship education, vision casting, and the promotion of a ministry need, such as a project that needs to be funded. All three are necessary. You are competing against all the rest of the "stuff" they are getting from the secular world, as well as other Christian organizations. Don't assume that your people are "sold" on your vision and ministries. When they understand who they are as a ministry, where they are going and why, they will begin to join you in "owning" it and supporting it. They want to feel they are part of a winning team. You need to communicate and promote this constantly. Again, remember the principle of *repetition*.

Activating Your Agenda

So, how do you weave all of this together? Where do you start? What would be a suggested agenda to follow? Much of *what you do* and *when you do it* will depend on the size and culture of your church or school. It will depend on how ready your leadership, including your pastoral or school staff, is to commit to a stewardship/generosity ministry. Are they open to engaging the services of a professional ministry qualified to help them get started? Ask them these questions:

- What are the demographics of our church? Are we a young church, with mostly young families and newer believers? Or, are we a large, more mature church?

- What is our ethnic mix and culture?
- How mature, spiritually, are our lay leaders?
- And what is our potential for forming our stewardship/ generosity ministry leadership team?
- Who will train them?
- Should we seek some professional help and training?
- Are we starting from scratch, or do we already have some experience with providing some classes or seminars on money management and financial planning?
- How generous are our people in the areas of time, talent and treasure?
- How fast do we want to get going?

Wherever you start, your people need to perceive that you are truly helping them grow spiritually as well as inviting them to become a part of the church or school vision in their stewardship. You don't want to give them the impression that you are just "getting them" to support the budget.

And, of course, bathe the whole effort in **prayer**. Have your prayer groups and leadership spend several weeks praying over your anticipated ministry effort. Complete and evaluate the results of the three surveys – the *Stewardship/Generosity Questionnaire*, the *Stewardship/Generosity Survey*, and for churches, *Your Church's Giving Potential Worksheet*. The results of these surveys will help you decide your agenda.

What to Pray For

- Finding the right lay leaders for your stewardship/ generosity leadership team.
- Wisdom in developing the best agenda of activities and events to start with.
- Strong support from your staff and lay leadership.

- Prepared hearts in your people to be receptive to future efforts and teaching on stewardship and generosity principles.

A Sample Two-year Agenda – To help you visualize what a "typical" stewardship/generosity ministry looks like, I have given you here a *sample* two-year agenda for just a church. It will also give you an idea of how to develop a possible agenda for a business or school environment. Keep in mind that this is just a *sample,* knowing that churches and other organizations differ. And, be advised that it will probably take longer than you think to train and bring your staff and lay stewardship/generosity ministry leadership team to a high level of knowledge and experience. This will be a *paradigm shift* for most of them. In getting started, you may only want to plan a year at a time, even though it will most likely take longer before you start seeing solid results. Here is the *sample* church agenda, put in the 'first' person:

FIRST LUTHERAN CHURCH – Any Town, USA

Stewardship/Generosity Ministry *AGENDA*

FIRST SIX MONTHS
1. Pray for and carefully recruit **candidates** for our lay stewardship/generosity ministry leadership team. TAKE OUR TIME in order to find the right people. This could take several months, as we will want to interview them and vet them regarding their qualifications, work ethic, and passion for this unique ministry. There also are resources available to allow us to test them for their gift-set, spiritual gifts, personality profile etc. in order to know which position on the leadership team fits their capabilities. (I list where you can obtain those resources at the end of Chapter Five and in Appendix One).
2. Once our lay stewardship/generosity leadership team is selected, we now need to train them. A good place to start

is to give each of them a copy of this book, meeting every two weeks with them to discuss the contents. We can also hire some professional ministry help for this responsibility. (I list some resources for this at the end of Chapter Five and in Appendix One).

3. We also need to "brief" our staff and church lay leadership team. We need to have them read this book and provide some briefing sessions and discussions so that they are 100% on board.

4. Next we will survey our congregation using the *Stewardship/Generosity Questionnaire,* and tabulate the results.

5. From the results of the questionnaire we will complete the *Stewardship/Generosity Survey and* complete *Your Church's Giving Potential Worksheet.*

6. From our evaluation of the *Stewardship/Generosity Survey* and *Your Church's Giving Potential Worksheet*, along with the church master calendar, we will schedule our first 6 to 12 month's *agenda.*

7. To start things off, we will have our pastor **preach** a series on biblical stewardship and generosity.

8. A week into the sermon series, during our worship service(s), we will **introduce** our lay stewardship and generosity ministry leadership team. We will share our vision for a stewardship/generosity ministry for the church. We will have several members of our team give brief testimonies of why they are a part of this emphasis. We will have our pastor speak on it as well. And then we will announce our first event or activity; a *budgeting class* in this sample. (I list ministries offering budgeting classes in Appendix Two).

SECOND SIX MONTHS

9. We will introduce our stewardship/generosity *column* in our **newsletter**. Our *Communications* leader can direct this by setting a schedule of selected copy, including

downloading from some listed websites and copy listed in Appendix One.

10. We will now start our *"stewardship moments"* in our worship services. We will draw copy from the resources listed in Appendix One and on our website, plus set up a monthly schedule of what each "moment" will be and who will conduct it. We will coordinate this schedule with our worship leader. (Mix verses, quotes and personal testimonies on stewardship and generosity each week).

11. As we approach the end of *year one*, we will want our pastor to **preach** another stewardship and/or generosity series. During his/her second series, we will approach our **adult Sunday school or discipleship class** leaders about offering a series on stewardship and/or generosity that follows the outline and theme contained in our pastor's preaching.

NOTE: Another *option* to this approach is to promote the series to the **whole church**, targeting those many folks who attend a worship service but are not connected to a Sunday school or discipleship class. Arrange with each class to "host" the series. This not only provides training for their class members, but can also attract some of those "not connected" group to their adult classes. It can be a win-win experience. At the conclusion of each series, members can be asked to complete a simple commitment card for their *next step* in stewardship and generosity education and ministry involvement. Ask the leaders of your church's various ministries, such as children's ministry, prayer, or worship to give you a list of *"resource needs"*, such as sponsors, teachers, or drivers. Then give that list to those who have completed the series, asking them to consider a commitment to one of those needs. You can make up a commitment card similar to this sample one:

> **Your NEXT STEP?** (check one or more)
>
> - Start a budget and work it
> - Get a will
> - Start tithing
> - Enroll in Small Group Study
> - Volunteer to teach Sunday school
> - Take Spiritual Gifts test
> - Train to be a budget counselor
>
> Name _____
> Phone _____
> E-mail _____

12. During our pastor's new sermon series, we will consider having our ***drama group*** (if you have one) create a presentation to help promote the series along with the Sunday school and/or discipleship class effort.
13. We will also introduce stewardship/generosity education into our ***new member's class***, drawing from our own resources by now or what is provided in Appendix One.
14. Before the end of the first year we will want to consider scheduling some type of ***seminar*** like basic ***financial and estate planning***. We will offer this at least once a year. (NOTE: You probably have access to local financial professional talent who can conduct the seminar. Later, in Chapter Four, I provide some basic ideas and guidelines for conducting a church-wide seminar).

SECOND YEAR – FIRST SIX MONTHS
15. We will encourage our pastoral staff to include some basic stewardship and generosity education when providing ***pre-marital counseling***. We will have these couples sign up for

either a small group financial Bible study or receive some instruction in a Sunday school class or seminar. This could end up being the best advice and training they receive to their new life together!

16. By now, it may be time to recruit some experienced people either from our stewardship/generosity ministry leadership team or who have led a small group financial bible study for our group of *personal financial counselors*. They should be invited to take a special course that prepares them to meet individually with needy couples or singles guiding them toward debt reduction and budgeting. This is a very time-intensive ministry and should only be attempted if we have enough counselors who are willing to give the necessary time. We will not broadcast this service until we have enough trained counselors to accept the potential requests for help. For individuals struggling with *excessive credit debt*, we will refer them to a credit counseling or debt reduction ministry in our area.

17. When our church holds its own *retreats*, we will not forget to include stewardship and generosity education occasionally as one of our "breakout" sessions. We can also use an invited guest speaker with experience in teaching an aspect of stewardship and generosity.

SECOND YEAR – SECOND SIX MONTHS

18. We are approaching the end of the second year, and it is now time to introduce stewardship and generosity into our *youth and children's ministries*. We will want to teach them while they are young and impressionable so they, hopefully, will not make the same mistakes we adults have. Some sources of materials for these groups are listed in Appendix Two. We will want to work closely with our youth and children's pastors or lay staff. We will let them study the material and decide how they will want to present it. They may decide to teach it in a Sunday group setting or small groups.

(NOTE: A great idea is to **teach parents** to use the materials to **teach their children**. This approach is excellent and effective because both the parent and child learn these truths, and additionally a wonderful bond is strengthened between parent and child).

19. We will start giving **ministry reports** in our written material as well as part of our worship service "stewardship moments," including the use of video. Our people need to hear about the results and blessings of their giving. We need to do what Para-church ministries do to communicate exciting results to their donors. We should not assume that our people know what God is doing through the ministries of our church. **We need to tell our story!**

20. Along with our ministry reports, we will **start thanking our people**. We will find creative ways to thank our people, either corporately or individually. We are reminded how profusely these para-church ministries and educational institutions are in thanking their donors for their financial support. Have your pastor make personal calls and visits to those faithful givers. We will keep in mind that a "sacrificial" gift could come from one of our poorer members. While thanking them, we will recast our vision, and ask them for prayer requests.

21. Since our church has ministry displays in the patio or foyer, we will have a **monthly stewardship and generosity display** or table, or do it during a special promotion of some stewardship activity such as a seminar or the next series of small group financial bible studies. (NOTE: This can be very effective in keeping the subject before your people. Always try to have someone from your stewardship/ generosity leadership team at your ministry display).

22. We will ask the church to include a **line item** on our church budget for a stewardship/generosity ministry in order to pay for our activities.

END OF SAMPLE AGENDA.

NOTE: As mentioned before, many of the items listed in this *Two-year Agenda* SAMPLE, including the *more activities* listed below, can be utilized or modified for use within a business or school setting. Here are a few *more activities* to possibly include during these two years:

- Make regularly scheduled *visits* to planned giving prospects. Assuming you have someone qualified to discuss with a church or school member the concept of a planned gift (more about this later), include your pastor or top leader in these visits. Remind him/her to mail a personal letter to each prospect visited thanking them for their time and encouraging them to consider what was discussed.

- Have a "Make Your Will Month" to encourage folks to get a *will or trust* and possibly include a charitable bequest for the church. Typically only about 5-10% of those with a will or trust include a charitable bequest.

- Stock and open your *library* for your people to check out stewardship books and materials. Advertise it in your newsletter or worship folder.

- If you hold a ministry and/or missions *fair*, include representatives from your stewardship/generosity leadership team.

- Conduct a *spiritual gifts* class or seminar.

- Have an active stock *brokerage account* for the church or school.

Finally, as you approach the end of the second year, it is time to *evaluate* how you are doing. Go through the following *checklist* to evaluate your progress:

Stewardship/Generosity Ministry Evaluation *Checklist*

- How many people have received stewardship and generosity instruction in our adult classes and what instructions were given? _____

_____

_____

- How many have been through a small group study and how many groups have been held? _____
  _____

- How well is our pastor or key leader providing effective leadership for our stewardship/generosity ministry through:
    - Preaching or teaching on stewardship and generosity? _____
    - Promoting its events? _____
    - Telling how God is using member's giving?
      _____

- Are we including a stewardship/generosity education column in our newsletter? Explain: _____
  _____

- How are we involving our new people in our stewardship/generosity ministry? _____
  _____

- How many seminars have we held? _____
  _____

- Which ones? _____
  _____

- Are we holding stewardship and/or generosity "moments" just before taking the offering during our worship services? Explain. _____
  _____

- How have we informed our people about Estate Planning and Deferred Gift Planning options and given them an opportunity to exercise those options? _____
  _____
  _____

- Knowing that most members will not grow in giving unless asked, how effectively have we challenged them to grow in their stewardship of:
    - Time? _____
    - Talents? _____
    - Treasure? _____
- How much has annual income increased to the church or school? $_____%_____
- How are we doing with teaching our youth and children in the area of stewardship & generosity? _____

_____

Stewardship/Generosity Ministry Agenda *Calendar*

I have provided on our website, www.visionresourcinggroup.com/free(book)resources.com   (or scan the QR code on your Smart Phone provided on the first page of Appendix One), a *sample* of a basic agenda calendar that you can edit for your own use to place your scheduled activities and events. One has a sample schedule marked in selected date boxes, and the second one is blank for you to copy and paste. Yours will be tailored to your specific agenda. Be sure to coordinate with your organization's master calendar to avoid conflicts. List all the possible activities you would like to commit to over the next two years and check the monthly boxes and years you want to engage in them in the sequence that fits your organization's needs and capabilities.

To summarize, in this Chapter, you learned of the possible activities, events and areas of church, business or school ministry that provide some aspect of stewardship and generosity education. I also gave you a *sample* two-year church agenda to help you visualize what a typical stewardship/generosity ministry could look like. I have also provided online a *sample* Agenda *Calendar,* one with activities marked in date boxes, and one kept blank for you to copy and paste. Remember the *analogy* of the organizational "water system" that provides multiple "faucets" where your people can "drink" or learn God's blessing of becoming a mature biblical steward and generous giver. As you form and schedule your tailored agenda of activities, the hearts and actions of your people will *begin to change*, gradually changing the giving culture of your organization. The resourcing of your vision will grow. Be patient; it will happen!

> *We proclaim him, admonishing and teaching everyone with all wisdom, so that we may present everyone perfect in Christ. To this end I labor, struggling with all his energy, which so powerfully works in me. (Colossians 1:28-29)*

CHAPTER FOUR –

HOW TO INTEGRATE SPECIFIC ACTIVITIES

In addition to providing you with some motivational reasons and general guidance to successfully implement a stewardship/generosity ministry, I want to give you some guidance on **utilizing specific teaching methods and venues** (Obviously, some apply more to a non-profit organization):

SEMINARS, SPECIAL EVENTS & CAMPAIGNS

SEMINARS

Seminars are an exceptionally good source for stewardship and generosity education, because they allow you to pack a lot of information into a short period of time. You can focus on specific topics and gain greater attention from those attending. You will want one of your Team members to give leadership to coordinating, promoting and conducting seminars. The actual teaching of the seminar may be a video or live presentation by trained professionals. Usually there are Christian financial planners and estate planning attorneys in your church or community who may be available to conduct these seminars.

There are also excellent live and video-driven seminars provided by the ministries listed in Appendix Two. You can contact these ministries for details and availability.

Organizing, Promoting, and Conducting a Seminar

- Charge a reasonable fee (unless you are offering it as a service to your employees, such as at lunch-time) to at least cover your costs. This also motivates people to show up and pay closer attention. I recommend that you insist upon payment along with a pre-registration slip during your promotional period. Don't tell them they can pay at the door if they want to. Experience has shown that almost 100% "show" with this policy. Otherwise, if you don't, you will have a lot of "no-shows" after you have committed to so many for refreshments, etc. Obviously, if someone should show up at the door without paying, collect their money and let them in. But this is the exception that you don't advertise.

- You may teach a seminar topic that requires the use of a professional financial planner and/or estate-planning attorney; or you can use an individual who is not in the business of offering financial and legal counsel. However, you should invite a licensed professional to assist or co-teach which lends credibility and technical assistance. It also introduces the students to professional help for subsequent follow-up implementation after the seminar. This helps provide motivation for those attending the seminar to follow through with their financial or estate planning needs.

- For seminars teaching subjects requiring financial or legal knowledge, offer a free consultation to all who want it following these seminars. In addition to using the instructor for this, assuming he or she has the time or ability, ask the assisting professionals to provide a free initial consultation. This is a very important service, and will motivate more to attend and follow through with what they need to do.

- In selecting professionals for assistance, you will want to be careful. Look for spiritual maturity, if they are Christians, and for professional competence. Look for proper motivation. You want someone who truly sees this as a ministry to your people not just an opportunity to acquire business. Interview them carefully, and make sure they understand your goals and requirements. It is imperative that you tell them *not* to collect any fee up front, such as a retainer fee, at their first free consultation with seminar attendees. You don't want a potential problem with a professional to backfire on your church or organization.

- For those seminars focusing more on biblical truths of stewardship and generosity, you may have one of your pastoral staff or a hired consultant conduct the seminar.
- Have a refreshment committee provide refreshments according to the time element of the seminar. It could involve a meal.
- Assign someone to handle pre-registrations. Participants can mail or turn in their registrations in person, sign up at a registration table Sunday mornings, or register online at your website.
- Consider organizing a phone committee to call people in the church or organization about the seminar, or just those who have pre-registered to remind them of when it starts, what to bring, and where it will be held.
- You might want to provide nursery care, although it is not always necessary.

Duties of the Seminar Chairperson

- Coordinate the scheduling of the various parts of the seminar with the church or organization calendar. Make certain there are no conflicts.
- Oversee the timely implementation of each promotion activity.
- Recruit other individuals to assist you. ***Don't try to do it alone***.
- Keep the organization's leadership informed and reminded of promoting events for which he/she is responsible.
- Recruit and coordinate the pre-registration for the seminar.
- Keep an accounting of registration funds and seminar expenses.
- MC the seminar program.
- Ensure that refreshments or meals are served during the seminar breaks.

Promotion Ideas

- Make up brochures (or flyers) and posters giving the details of the seminar. Some seminar resource ministries will supply you with these, depending on the subject matter being taught.
- The brochure or flyer should have a "tear-off" pre-registration slip.
- Use a pre-seminar survey sheet to help stir interest as well as to give you an idea of what their felt-need is. You can have folks complete them and turn them in right away. Then tally the results to give to your presenter. Here is a *sample* that you can copy, shorten and/or modify:

Financial and Estate Planning Survey

Please check off your **PRIORITY** questions and concerns listed below regarding personal financial and estate planning. This will help the presenters of the up-coming seminar know which material to emphasize for your benefit. **THANKS!**

1. _____How can I get better control of my spending and reduce expenses?
2. _____How do I get out of debt?
3. _____When is it OK for a Christian to declare bankruptcy?
4. _____What are some common financial mistakes?
5. _____How can I minimize my taxes?
6. _____When is it better to have a Living Trust instead of a Will?
7. _____What is probate and how can I avoid it?
8. _____How do I maximize my investment growth and minimize my risk?
9. _____How do I save and plan for retirement?
10. _____What is a proper insurance strategy for me and my family?
11. _____Why does God want me to give?
12. _____Should I tithe to the church?
13. _____How do I protect my assets from possible long-term care expenses?
14. _____How can I give to the Lord's work after I die?

- Include some "teasers" in your worship folder or communication pieces along with written announcements. Here are some *samples* to give you some ideas. You will want to write them for the specific seminar you are promoting:

- Are you in debt? Want to know how to get out? Register for the upcoming Financial & Estate Planning seminar ___ (time/date)____at the church.
- Do you find that you have more "month" than money left at the end of the month? For help, register for the upcoming Financial & Estate Planning seminar __(time/date)_____at the church.
- What does God teach us in His Word about how to manage our money? Find out at the upcoming "Managing Your Money God's Way" _____ (time/date)___ at the church.
- How much insurance is enough? How do you design the most cost-effective insurance plan for your needs? Find out at the upcoming Financial & Estate Planning seminar __ (time/date) _____at the church.
- What are good investment principles and strategies? What does the Bible say? Find out at the upcoming Financial & Estate Planning seminar _____ (time/date)_____at the church.
- What happens if I die without a will? Who will take care of my children? Who will receive my estate? Find out at the upcoming Financial & Estate Planning seminar __ (time/date) _____at the church.
- How can I avoid probate? Is that a good idea? Find out at the upcoming Estate Planning seminar __ (time/date)_____at the church.
- Should I have a will or living trust? How do I know which is best for me? Find out at the upcoming Estate Planning seminar __ (time/date)_____at the church.

- How can I protect my assets from the high cost of long-term care? Find out at the upcoming Advanced Tax & Estate Planning seminar _____ (time/date)____ at the church.
- How can I make estate and capital gain taxes "optional"? Find out at the upcoming Advanced Tax & Estate Planning seminar _____ (time/date)____ at the church.
- How can I increase my retirement income through charitable giving? Find out at the upcoming Advanced Tax & Estate Planning seminar _____ (time/date)____ at the church.

Pre-Seminar Promotion Events/Timeline

- **Eight** or more weeks ahead - Set the seminar date; recruit leader team or committee; arrange for room, audio-visual equipment, sound system, refreshments and/or lunch.
- **Seven** weeks prior to seminar - Start including "teasers" in worship folder or communication pieces.
- **Six** weeks prior to seminar date - Put up posters.
- **Five** weeks prior to seminar date - Pastor or leader letter mailed out or inserted in newsletter, if published, to promote seminar.
- **Four** weeks prior to seminar date – Verbal announcements begin.
- **Three** weeks prior to seminar date - Seminar pre-registration brochures and surveys distributed along with verbal announcements. Collect the completed surveys that day to insure that you get the information you want!
- **Two** weeks prior to seminar date - Pre-registration brochures distributed along with verbal announcements.
- **One** week prior to seminar date - Same as two weeks prior to seminar.

- **Week of seminar** - Phone all pre-registrants to remind/confirm their attendance. Confirm that all physical arrangements, refreshments and equipment are prepared.
- **Day of seminar** - Have team arrive one hour early to set up.

Set-up the day of the seminar - Check to ensure the following:

- Adequate seating and tables to write on, lighting, climate control, marker board
- Table in front to hold audio-visual equipment, presenter's materials; podium
- Registration table for handing out any materials, tracking of those who pre-registered, and collection of any late registration money.
- Book table if you choose to sell books dealing with topics covered.
- Refreshments (for breaks and lunch if provided).
- Directional signs outside to guide people to room.

Conducting the Seminar

- Greet people as they enter and confirm their pre-registration payment (checks should be made out to the organization)
- Hand out any seminar materials, such as student notes, to each person attending.
- Hand out a registration form (see sample below) to each family "unit." This provides you with a record of who attended, and if printed on NCR paper, allows them to record the day and time of their follow-up consultation appointment if taken.
- Have them take a seat and complete the registration form.
- Welcome the people; opening prayer; introduce the instructor(s).

- Brief them on the schedule, bathroom locations and any other administrative details.
- Explain how to sign up for their free consultation during the breaks (if you are providing one).
- Be prepared during the breaks to help people sign up for their free consultation (if you are providing one) at the registration table. Provide sign-up sheets listing the days and hours available for those conducting the consultations. The people should be given a reminder slip or card as to when and where they will have their consultation.

Follow-up To the Seminar

- If the consultations are to be held at the church, arrange to have a room available with a table and three chairs. It should provide good privacy. In some cases, the people will meet with the professionals at their offices.
- Appointments can be scheduled from 9 a.m. to 6 p.m. with 90 minutes allowed for each, plus time for a lunch break. This allows for six appointments per day. Let the professionals and their schedules guide you with this.
- Have the church secretary type up a master list of those who attended the seminar.
- You can use the *sample* seminar registration form below at any of your seminars if you plan on offering free personal consultations after the seminar. It also serves as a record of those who attended. An option is to print it on NCR paper so you can leave copies with attendees to remind them of their appointment, the person scheduling appointments, and the consultants who will be meeting with the attendees.

Seminar Registration Form (please print)

Name _____

Seminar location _____

Address _____

E-mail _____

Seminar date/time _____

Phone (bus.) (_____ **)** _____

(res.) (_____ **)** _____

FREE Initial Consultation Appointment

Date___ / ___ / ___   Time_____a.m./p.m.

LOCATION:
- **Church** _____
- **Other** _____
- **Please call me for an appointment after the following date:** ____ / ____ / ____

WHAT TO BRING: The completed Personal Financial & Estate Planning Forms given to you. Even though there is no charge for the initial consultation, time has been reserved for your appointment, and it is very important that you notify the church or individual if a change in appointment is needed. **THANK YOU!**

SPECIAL EVENTS & CAPITAL FUND CAMPAIGNS

Your comprehensive stewardship/generosity ministry will most likely, at some time, include scheduling a *Special Event* and/or *Capital Fund Campaign*. Presented here are some selected ideas, principles, and outlines for conducting church special events and capital fund campaigns. Due to the potential volume of material and consultants available on these topics, our goal here is to give you some *general guidelines* and possibly help get you started. Once you decide what you want to accomplish, you need to research organizations and consulting services that can give you more detail and assistance. I've listed a few organizations and consultants in Appendix Two. Obviously, you can locate others off the Internet or referrals from a stewardship and generosity ministry consultant you may hire.

Special Events

Special events can be for any number of projects or needs from an annual stewardship campaign, raising money to send out a missionary, to providing scholarship money for high school students to attend summer camp. They can be organization-wide in scope or within a special ministry of your organization. It usually is a smaller event rather than a large capital improvement campaign and may last only a few weeks. It may only involve a special dinner to make a presentation. The *types* of special events may be:

- A *banquet* at the end of a period of promotion is the most labor/time intensive event, but can expose your whole membership to your fund-raising event.
- A *briefing* over lunch or dinner, by special invitation is much easier to plan and can vary in size. Keep it under 30 people.
- *Home gatherings*, very small and intimate with one host, are easiest to plan, and they are the most informal.

- *Collection cans* distributed to families to put their excess change in each day.
- A *matching gift* program where the church seeks special gifts to match a pre-committed gift in order to double the final gift. For example, a major donor in the church could promise to give $10,000 toward a special project for the high school ministry if the high school students and families raise $10,000, making the total gift $20,000.

Experience has shown that over time, as a church or non-profit organization implements a stewardship/generosity ministry, they will not have to rely as much on special events every time they need money for certain projects. They will not have to put as much effort into their special events. This is because as the people grow in their stewardship discipleship, generosity and giving commitment, they will more readily give to the needs of the organization when they are presented. Sometimes just a solid and exciting report on a given ministry opportunity and request to fund it will be enough.

Putting the "Special" into Special Events [2] - Here are five key elements to help you experience successful special events:

- Events, like the organizations that sponsor them, must have a *clear mission*. It's imperative that the planning committee and staff are focused on the objectives for:
    - Attendance—Who and how many do we want to attend?
    - Outcome—What are we trying to achieve?
    - Audience involvement—What do we want people to do?

---

2 Don Goehner, President of Goehner Resource Group, San Jose, CA; Article in the Spring 1997 issue of their *Resource Concepts* newsletter. Used by permission.

- The best special events **make the purpose of the occasion very clear** to the invited guests, whether it is to raise funds, introduce people to a new program, or present a new opportunity for their involvement.
- *Timing*, as they say, is everything. An event lasting longer than two hours is likely to lose its impact. The difference between a two-hour program and a two-hour and thirty-minute program can often result in thousands of dollars of unrealized revenue. People are extremely time-conscious, very busy in their daily lives and their family commitments. When event managers honor their guests' time constraints by beginning and concluding their events on time, attendees will appreciate it, and respond to solicitations accordingly.
- There must be clear *communication* with the guests regarding the purpose of the event. Be sure to inform your guests *prior* to a fund-raising event that a specific request for funds will be made. No one likes to be surprised, and most people are already suspect of fund-raising efforts without aggravating the situation with a murky message about the true reason for the event.
- *Motivated, trained volunteers* are the best fund-raisers. Furthermore, the best fund-raising or special events involve dozens of volunteers. People come to, or avoid, events because of who invites them. Use a guest-host strategy, resulting in friends inviting friends to a location that has the feel of someone's living room, rather than an impersonal meeting room.
- *Quality* is mandatory in all aspects of the event. By that I mean:
  - Attractive and error-free printed materials
  - An excellent video or multi-media presentation
  - Good food
  - A first-class location
  - An outstanding program

When you combine these features with hosts who are committed to your cause and a staff that produces an outstanding program clarifying your mission, your event will validate your commitment to quality and help achieve your goals. Special events should be exactly that, special. Doing them right is a matter of planning, attention to detail and good oversight, not chance. The rewards— for both audience and organization—are well worth the effort.

If you conduct *Annual Stewardship Campaigns,* here are Eight Planning Components for an Effective one. [3]

1. **Creating Vision**
   - What is the scope of ministry of our membership for the upcoming year?
   - What excites us?
   - What will excite other members and friends about the ministries of our church or organization?
   - What are the distinctive elements of our organization?
   - How will we emphasize them during the coming year?

2. **Gathering Information**
   - What does our membership need to understand in order to make informed decisions about their support of our ministries?
   - How will the necessary information be gathered, and how can it be conveyed to both the heads and hearts of members and friends?

3. **Establishing a Theological Foundation**
   - How will Scripture inform us to grow as stewards of the resources God has given to us?

---

[3] Sanford D. Coon, Stewardship Consultant with the Texas Methodist Foundation. Notes from his workshop at the 1998 Christian Stewardship Association Annual Conference.

- What is the particular biblical passage, story, or verse upon which the campaign will be built that will give the endeavor faithful relevance and focus the thrust and vitality of the campaign?
- Is there a biblical truth that can become a viable theme of the campaign or framework for it?

4. **Planning our Intensive Phase**
   - How will the information about the projected ministries be communicated in ways that are personalizing and that emerge from our theological foundation?
   - What time period will be our primary, intensive phase of the emphasis? What needs to be done prior to that in order to have maximum impact during the intensive phase?
   - How will members and friends be invited to respond and make their commitments?
   - What reluctance can we expect from members, and how will we address those issues?
   - What questions do we anticipate, and how will we answer them?

5. **Mobilizing Our Resources**
   - Who will need to do what and when in order to implement the process we have devised?
   - How much will it cost, and how will it be paid for? (At least one percent)
   - What system of accountability will we have to assure that tasks are completed on schedule and that costs are within our guidelines?

6. **Conveying Inspiration**
   - What will inspire members and friends to engage in the campaign, to devotedly reflect and discern how God would have them respond in commitment?

7. **Anticipating Celebration**
   - How will we bring joyful, celebrative completeness to our endeavors that will be appropriate to the culture of our organization, authentic to our scriptural heritage, and inspiring to our members as a whole?

8. **Remaining Thankful**
   - How will we acknowledge every commitment made to the projected ministries of the organization?
   - Is our financial record keeping effective and efficient, or do we need to make changes before we begin our new fiscal year?
   - How will we maintain the flow of current, accurate, motivational and legally compliant information about individual, family and member support throughout the year?

Here are some Additional Ideas for an Annual Stewardship Campaign[4]

1. **Plan, Plan, Plan!** An Annual Stewardship Campaign requires foresight and planning. Hastily concocted campaigns tend to produce limited or disappointing results. An effective campaign is developed simultaneously on many fronts so that the membership is informed, primed and ready to make their commitments because of weeks of prayerful, familial, and personal preparation.
2. **Listen to the Professionals**. Keep it positive, biblical, and stress the mission.
3. **Determine the Best Season for Your Campaign.**
4. **People give to Ministries, not Budgets**. Emphasize ministry awareness and challenge growth in faithful stewardship. Tell stories of what God is doing.

---

[4] Dr. Michael Reeves, president, United Methodist Foundation of Louisiana.

5. **Prepare a Narrative Budget**. A narrative budget describes the ministries of the organization in an informative and inviting way. It describes in "humanizing" fashion how the organization is fulfilling its God-given mission.
6. **Show Your Stuff**. Schedule a Ministry Fair or Missions Fair. Present by videotape, slides, music and computer-generated graphics a multimedia presentation during morning worship.
7. **Involve People**. The more people that are involved in the planning and preparation of the Annual Stewardship Campaign, the more ownership there is for the campaign and its objectives.
8. **Plan Your Commitment Card**. Make it work for your situation.
9. **Let the Leaders Lead**. Invite them to make their commitment a few days prior to Commitment Day. Then, prior to or at the Commitment Day services, announce the total of the commitments being made by leaders (a good passage on this is 1 Chronicles 29:2-9).
10. **Describe Ways Gifts Can be Made**. Encourage people to consider making their gift with appreciated stock or other types of planned gifts.
11. **Give a Final Report**. Following Commitment Day, allow an interval of about two weeks before giving a final report to the membership.
12. **Interpret the Results**. Use some means to interpret the outcome of the campaign. Provide an overall percentage of growth in comparison to the previous fiscal year, and describe how the ministries and programs of the church or organization will be strengthened and expanded as a result.
13. **Say Thank You**. A letter to each individual and/or family unit that has made a commitment can convey gratitude and verify the amount of the commitment and the intervals when it will be fulfilled, such as weekly, monthly, or quarterly.

14. **Insist on Accuracy of Records**. Before mailing anything, check and re-check that names, address, commitment amount and other information is accurate.

Here are a few basic principles to follow when conducting a banquet or event

1. **Networking**
   - Each table is a **circle of friends**, meaning that they have been invited by their friend, the table host.
   - People attend because of **relationships**. Try to get your event supporters to invite their friends, not strangers. Their potential response to an appeal will be greater if their host demonstrates a commitment to the project or need.
   - Emphasis on reaching new people. Have your table hosts seek to invite new people to get them involved.

2. **Honest Personal Approach**
   - Honest explanation of purpose of banquet or event. People want to know and need to know the exact purpose. This prepares their hearts when they arrive.
   - Personal invitation by letter **and** phone. Do not depend on people responding to a letter only. A few rare individuals will, but most will need that personal, verbal touch.
   - Attempt to make the event personal. This just means to be yourself; create an atmosphere that demonstrates an honest, relaxed environment. This is another reason why you put friends of each host at the same table.

3. **Emphasis on Quality and Brevity**
   - You need a quality location, quality meal, and a quality program.

- Brevity of the event. including the program, is important. Prepare everyone involved in the program to ensure you stay on schedule.

4. **Commitment of Volunteers**
   - You need committed volunteers for your ministry. Don't be so "hungry" for volunteers that you recruit individuals who are not 100% committed to your ministry, project or reason for the special event. Go for quality over quantity.
   - Encourage volunteers to inform and challenge new friends. "Stretch" your volunteers to reach out.
   - Make sure your volunteers are educated in sound biblical stewardship. They need to be well informed and properly trained.

Capital Fund Campaigns

Seven Keys to Conducting Successful Church Building Projects [5]

(Highlights of nationwide interviews with 15 churches that conducted successful building fund drives)

The Importance of Instructing and Inspiring

LESSON #1—*PROVIDE BIBLICAL TEACHING*: Most churches found that their people were in need of practical and inspirational instruction and encouragement in the areas of Christian giving and stewardship. Churches found it helpful and very important that these areas be taught from the pulpit by the Senior Pastor and/or an experienced stewardship speaker so that a proper spiritual tone and biblical basis was established for the drive.

LESSON #2—*INCLUDE PERSONAL TESTIMONIES*: A number of churches actively included personal testimonies during worship

---

[5] Brian Kluth, *Stewardship Resource Manual*, Christian Stewardship Association. Used by permission.

times from people who have experienced the grace of giving in their lives and/or who were specifically led by the Lord to become supportive of the expansion project. Written testimonies, handouts, and articles were also used to help encourage people in the spiritual aspects of their giving decisions.

LESSON #3—AIM TO MAKE THE FUND DRIVE A RICH SPIRITUAL EXPERIENCE: Many churches indicated that their expansion drives helped deepen people's faith and spiritual commitment (i.e., especially through the increased vision people received, the interaction people had with others during the drive, and/or their increased or sacrificial giving to the Lord's work at the church).

The Importance of Identifying & Informing

LESSON #4—HAVE A COMPREHENSIVE PLAN: Every successful funding effort had a specific plan on how they were going to instruct, inspire, inform and appropriately involve people within the following groups:

- LEADERSHIP: Pastors, staff, key leaders of ministries and committees.
- ACTIVE MEMBERSHIP: People regularly involved in serving in the church.
- POTENTIAL MAJOR GIVERS: People who exhibited the gift of giving in the past or who may have the potential to be a major financial help in the drive.
- REGULAR ATTENDERS: People who attend church at least twice a month.
- FRINGE PEOPLE: Occasional or sporadic attendees.

LESSON #5—GET EXPERIENCED HELP: In addition to the active involvement of many lay leaders and present staff, nearly all the churches that raised major dollars for expansion efforts used some level of experienced help to lead them through the funding process.

LESSON #6—DEVELOP HELPFUL COLLATERAL MATER-IALS: Each church developed materials that effectively informed their congregation what the plans were and what level of help and support would be needed. Items often developed included multimedia presentations, case-statement brochures, question and answer flyers, personal presentation packets, commitment cards, mailings, and update sections in church publications.

The Importance of Inviting and Involving

LESSON #7—HAVE SPECIFIC COMMITMENT TIME(S): Following a period of advance instruction, inspiration and information, churches would invite their people to carefully and prayerfully indicate how the Lord has led them to be involved in the church expansion plans. In a number of cases this was done in two stages. The **first** stage would be receiving the commitments from the families that make up the church's main leadership and lead givers. The **second** phase (2-4 weeks later) would be receiving the commitments from the rest of the congregation on a specific target date or event.

"How to Determine When NOT to Build" [6] - (*Church Building Projects)*

Helpful questions for church leaders to consider

Answer the following questions about your church:

		Yes	No
1.	The regular giving in our church is strong.	☐	☐
2.	The giving units—individuals or families who give regularly—represent a majority of the congregation.	☐	☐

---

[6] *Stewardship Resource Manual,* Christian Stewardship Association. Taken from church architect Ray Bowman's book *When Not to Build,* Baker House Publishing. PP. 107-108

3. We consistently meet our budget, fully funding ☐ ☐
    our ministries and staff needs.

4. Our budget includes adequate funds for ☐ ☐
    intentional outreach to meet the needs of
    people in the community.

5. We teach biblical financial principles to our ☐ ☐
    families and individuals, including an emphasis
    on biblical giving.

6. The church is out of debt. ☐ ☐

7. Through the use of a building and funding ☐ ☐
    survey we have found out that the present
    giving units are ready to commit themselves to
    an increase in their giving to cover the cost of
    construction and future building operation costs
    so that none of the church's present ministry
    spending would ever have to be diverted to
    help cover the costs of the new building.

8. The increased giving for future facilities is ☐ ☐
    currently accumulating and is being wisely
    invested for a good return.

9. The church has enough invested in its building ☐ ☐
    fund to be able to pay cash or almost cash for
    the proposed building program.

Following these questions, Ray Bowman says, "If you checked yes
to the first 6 questions, your church is probably basically
financially healthy, and by implementing numbers 7, 8 and 9 you
should be financially ready to build within a few years. As soon as
all nine statements are true about your church, you have then
passed the financial readiness test and should proceed with your

building plans." *(NOTE: Brian Kluth, past President of the Christian Stewardship Association, says that this is an outstanding book. He says, "No church leadership board should consider any major renovation or building plans before each board member reads this book!")*

Financing your Building Project – HOW?

Here are 25 advantages of using prayerful planning and an orderly funding effort vs. long-term debt for your building and expansion needs [7]

In this "radical idea" article by Brian Kluth (www.kluth.org), he says, "I would like to share with you some of the specific *advantages* I have experienced with ministries and churches that decided **NOT** to use long-term borrowing (mortgages or bonds) to fund their expansion plans. They worked in an orderly manner to inform, inspire, instruct, and invite God's people to help pray for and provide the necessary resources to meet their building and expansion needs:

1. More people will be better informed, inspired and involved in the project.
2. A greater number of people will make specific financial commitments to the effort.
3. There will be a greater number of large and generous gifts given to the fund drive.
4. It will be easier to raise funds for something you are *going to do* than for *something you did*. It is always more exciting when people can give to the dream vs. having to pay off the debt.
5. You will not endanger the future of your normal ministry. As the ministry does grow, you will be in a stronger financial position to add needed programs or to fund additional staff.

---

[7] Brian Kluth, past President Christian Stewardship Association, *Stewardship Resource Manual.* (www.kluth.org) Used by permission.

6. You will be a witness to your community and to unbelievers about the power of God to provide.
7. You will be in harmony with all the biblical examples of building projects in the Scriptures (*They paid cash!*).
8. Other ministries who look up your ministry will be able to follow your model and example.
9. You will not be locked into any of the ups and downs of your city or country's economy.
10. You will not have to presume upon the future (things that you are hoping will happen or that will have to happen) in order to make required payments.
11. You will keep people more informed and there will be a greater need for prayer during times of specific need.
12. You will save hundreds of thousands of dollars in interest payments. For example, a 15-year mortgage at 10% interest requires you to pay $1 in interest for every building dollar you received! (*This article was written when interest rates were higher*)
13. You will have an ideal opportunity to teach and model to your people what the Scriptures teach about matters of stewardship, finances, giving and building.
14. People will be appropriately invited to make giving decisions according to the resources God has entrusted to them. These giving decisions will often result in an increase in their personal faith and trust in the Lord.
15. There will be a greater level of faith, excitement, and anticipation of how God will lead and provide.
16. The ministry's leadership will not have to violate the biblical principle of surety or cosigning (i.e., not having a "sure way" to pay, having to put up additional collateral, or the necessity for leaders to co-sign on the financing). This will keep you from becoming a slave to the lender.
17. You will likely see more of God's "creative provisions and miracles" to meet the specific needs you'll face along the way.

18. The project will be broken down into clearer stages and phases that have specific dollar needs that help people understand the importance and value of their gifts.
19. More people (from inside and outside of your ministry) will be inclined to donate or discount needed items, labor and services.
20. You will be more careful, prayerful, wise, and realistic about what items you should actually include in the fund drive.
21. You will find that you put to better use the gifts, skills and experiences of the people God has put in your ministry.
22. You will create long-term financial freedom for your ministry and you will not hinder your ongoing ministry or missions giving.
23. You will not only gain people's treasure, you will gain their hearts. This will greatly strengthen the depth and breadth of the body life in your church.
24. You will help more people make giving to the Lord a regular priority in their life.
25. And best of all, you will never regret the decision you made to **NOT** use long-term borrowing for your building needs.

THE ABC'S OF CHOOSING A CONSULTANT. Often a consultant is needed to help in the fundraising process. Here is advice on choosing one wisely:

A. Obviously, make sure the consultant is knowledgeable and experienced. Make sure the consultant's background, expertise and track record fits your situation as closely as possible.

B. Make sure he/she fits your ministry personality and style. When checking references, ask, "How well did the consultant fit in with you, your board, your staff and your donors?"

C. Realize that a successful campaign is a lot of hard work. The best consultant in the world cannot guarantee ultimate success and does not do all the work. At best he/she provides guidance, a framework for the campaign and gives needed counsel and encouragement.

When planning a campaign, here are some principles to keep in mind. (These are from Dr. Lou Petrie, former Vice-President, Ministry Advancement, Baptist General Conference, now CONVERGE)

- Plan a feasibility study. Examine all the factors and components carefully to determine what your possibilities are for success.
- A church that is healthy with a great mission and vision can expect to raise up to four times its annual budget over a 3-year period. For debt retirement it can expect to raise one and half to two times the annual budget over 3 years.
- A campaign is usually divided into two categories—the quiet phase (sometimes called the leadership phase) and the public phase. Most campaigns last 3 years, and it is anticipated through the quiet phase that at least 30%-50% of the needed amount in cash will be raised to lead the campaign into the public phase.
- A professional consultant will usually raise more money than a do-it-yourself campaign effort.
- The campaign needs to be based on prayer and hard work.

Two Common Fatal Flaws in Failed Building Programs[8]

FATAL FLAW #1 = **FALSE ASSUMPTIONS.** Church leaders assume everyone else knows what they know, dream like they dream, believe what they believe, and conclude what they conclude. By *asking questions* of your congregation, you discover where they really are.

---

[8] John H. Hewett, Ph.D., executive vice president of Cargill Associates, Ft. Worth, Texas. Taken from notes given at a workshop at the 1998 Christian Stewardship Association Annual Convention.

FATAL FLAW #2 = SHORTCUTS. A building process can be long and arduous. Shortcuts will hurt you at *three distinct points* in the process.

1. **The Conception Stage**—A few people supporting the project may lead us to *believe* that everyone wants it. Take time for others to understand and support the project.
2. **The Planning Stage**—Plans make the project more specific. They answer questions and create the vision. They also become the target for objections and misunderstanding. Careful planning, professionally guided, can be a vital investment in the future success of the project.
3. **The Final Strategy Stage**—The financial plans for a building project will impact the church and its future more than the actual design of the building. A congregation left in disarray or in severe debt can have a crippled ministry for many years. An initial investment of time to plan the financial strategy for a building project will pay enormous dividends in the future.

Why Should a Church Hire an Outside Consultant?[9]

- Most churches do not have staff or lay people with the time and expertise to design and direct an effective campaign. The task usually falls to the senior pastor, who can compromise his pastoral role as "the fund-raiser."
- A church stewardship consultant can positively influence the financial results of a capital campaign. Studies show that a typical consultant-directed campaign will raise 50% or more above a self-led campaign.
- An experienced stewardship consultant will bring a spiritual focus to a capital campaign.

---

[9] Dr. Michael Reeves, president, United Methodist Foundation. Used with permission.

- An experienced consultant will provide a well-organized and proven plan of action to reach the total congregation, involving and reaching people outside the faithful givers.
- A professional consultant will create a positive infrastructure of accountability in regards to the timely completion of assignments in the campaign.
- A consultant must only raise the amount of the fee, over what a church could raise on its own, to be a worthwhile investment. Campaign results show that the return will be many times more than the cost of professional services.

Choosing the Right Consultant for Your Campaign [10]

One of the most important and difficult decisions a church or consultant must make is the selection of a professional consultant. Here are some selected questions you should ask:

- Who is the on-site consultant responsible for our campaign?
- How many years of experience does the company have?
- How many years of experience does the consultant have who would be on-site to lead our campaign?
- How many campaigns has he/she conducted in churches similar in membership and annual budget to ours?
- How much time will this campaign take?
- Will this consultant conduct other campaigns at the same time?
- How will the campaign be developed and implemented to employ the unique features, distinctive needs and particular circumstances of our congregation?
- What kind of follow-up to the campaign is provided?
- What are the fees, and how are they paid?
- Identify the last three campaigns conducted by the consultant who would be conducting our campaign. Talk

---

[10] Ibid.

with those who worked with the consultant on those campaigns.

To summarize, you learned about the value of well-conducted seminars as part of your agenda. You learned how to promote and conduct them, along with offering personal follow-up appointments. I shared with you a few basic principles and suggestions to guide you as you engage in some form of a special event or capital campaign. It is beyond the scope of this book to give you a comprehensive manual on annual and capital campaigns. As you access consultants and resources listed in the back of the book for a stewardship/generosity ministry, you will have many choices to draw from as you seek assistance.

"Plans fail for lack of counsel, but with many advisers they succeed." (Proverbs 15:22)

CHAPTER FIVE –

HOW TO INTEGRATE ESTATE & GIFT PLANNING

Keep in mind, as emphasized earlier, that as you gradually help your people grow to stewardship and giving "maturity," their increased giving will provide the resources you need to fulfill your God-given vision. You will discover that you will need to rely less on campaigns and fund-raisers to resource your vision. Now, let's look at an often *overlooked* part of a successful stewardship/generosity ministry, *Estate and Gift Planning.*

Why You Should Include Estate & Gift Planning in Your Stewardship/Generosity Ministry

In 2 Kings 20:1, the prophet Isaiah came to King Hezekiah, saying, "Put your house in order, because you are going to die; you will not recover." Basically, God was telling Hezekiah to complete his estate planning, so that when he died, his wishes could be carried out by those who survived him. Proverbs 13:22 says, "A good man leaves an inheritance for his children's children". Estate planning is the process of planning your estate in such a way that after you die, it properly affects the people in your life, transfers your property efficiently while minimizing probate and tax expense and guides those who will assist you in achieving your goals. It involves the right legal documents that will direct those in the process of settling your estate. Included in this process is the opportunity to **leave a charitable gift**. This is the sacred privilege given us by God to continue giving to His kingdom ministries after we are gone. It allows you to control where that "social capital" goes that God has endowed to you. Many country's tax laws, including the United States, allow us to direct the giving of our "social capital" away from government control. We need to inform our church members of this opportunity and show them how to accomplish it.

> ***There are only three places to distribute your estate-***
>   ***1) Family and friends***
>   ***2) Charity and ministry***
>   ***3) Government***

What we are talking about here is an area of a stewardship/generosity ministry that most churches and many non-profit ministries are neglecting. It is the area of *planned giving*, which is a part of *financial and estate planning*. Planned giving refers primarily to "deferred gifts" after members die and go to be with the Lord, although it can refer to current gifts that require special legal and tax assistance. To get you started on this topic, answer these *two questions*:

- How many funerals of supporting members and attendees did your ministry hold the past five years?
- How much money was given to your church or ministry through those decedents' estate plans?

Chances are it was minimal. Statistics reveal that about 60 to 70% of Americans do *not* have a will or trust. Unfortunately, this is also representative of Christians. The **real tragedy** is that of those who *do* have a will or trust, approximately 5% remembered the Lord (including the church) in their estate plan. This is 5% of the 30 to 40% who *do* have a will or trust. Also, recognize that most deferred gifts are given upon the "second death," the death of the surviving spouse.

Missed Opportunities

Millions of dollars of "God's money" is "lost" to unbelieving heirs, secular entities and unnecessary taxes by sincere Christians because of no or poor financial and estate planning. Over the years the federal government has collected millions of dollars *per week* in estate (death) taxes from those who were unprepared to leave their possessions behind. For example, in 1990, the federal government collected $185,000,000 *per week*. Assuming that only ten percent of the people dying in 1990 were Christians, approximately $18,000,000 per week could have been directed to God-honoring people or programs, or both! Imagine what that figure would be today.

The minority of Christians who did include God's work in their estate plans often left it to a ministry other than their local church. Your people are being asked by other ministries and institutions to leave a portion of their estate to them when they die. This is wonderful, as it is still funding a portion of God's Kingdom. However, because most churches have no program to secure these planned gifts and bequests, people often forget to remember their own church. This does not have to be.

Experts estimate that between $10 and $45 **trillion** will be subject to estate transfer during the next 15 or 20 years, the largest transfer of wealth in the history of the world. If your church has a desire to benefit from special gifts, you need to provide an opportunity for your members to thoughtfully consider gift and estate planning options now.

The April, 1998 issue of *Give & Take Newsletter* states that "90% or more of charitable bequests and a large percentage of bequest dollars are realized from the estates of lower and middle income persons who are seeking to make their 'gift of a lifetime....'" Therefore, you don't have to have a large number of wealthy people in your congregation or membership to benefit from deferred giving since most charitable gifts come from individuals with average-sized estates.

Realistically, you are going to need some professional help to effectively implement an estate and gift planning capability within your stewardship/generosity ministry. But, to get you started, here is a **brief explanation** of what, why and how to do that:

What is planned giving? Planned giving is the process of placing those *gifts (current or deferred) that require special planning and/or handling to set up and complete.* These gifts often come from accumulated assets rather than current income and therefore, may be larger than gifts from current income. They may be present gifts for immediate use by a ministry, or deferred gifts for later use. Usually these involve an advanced application of estate and tax planning that requires licensed professionals and counsel. In addition to requiring special legal documents, it can include certain financial instruments in order to complete the gifting process.

Why you should include planned giving in your stewardship/Generosity ministry.

The following points should motivate you to include a planned giving program for your people, specifically your seniors:

- The percentage of people in North America 85 or older is increasing.
- In 1900 life expectancy was 46 years. In 2010 the average of all races was around 75 for men and around 80 for women.
- For most of us, a charitable bequest in our estate plan will be the largest gift we ever make.
- Most individuals are interested in providing a charitable bequest in their estate plan once they understand how and why to include it in their plan.
- Because of the potential size of a charitable bequest, it can give your organization a large sum to direct toward a major ministry need.
- A planned giving program in your stewardship/generosity ministry helps your people become better stewards of the estate God has given them to manage. It not only saves potential probate and estate taxes, it gives them peace and

joy knowing that their estate will help advance God's kingdom. It is a *win-win* situation.

Types of assets as planned gifts

- Securities, such as stocks, bonds, mutual funds
- Cash, such as certificates of deposits
- Real estate
- Life insurance and annuities
- Antiques, collectibles, art

TYPES OF PLANNED GIFTS:

Bequests

A bequest through a will or trust is the most common type of planned gift. Almost every adult should have a will or living trust, and every Christian should at least consider making a charitable gift through his or her estate. There is a scriptural, moral, and legal responsibility to provide for a spouse, minor-age children, and any others who may be dependent. For example, the church or other non-profit being supported by donors would qualify as one of those "dependents".

Since everything a person owns (during life and at death) belongs to God, a Christian should attempt to distribute their estate to family members, friends, and ministries that will use those assets in a way that honors the Lord.

A gift through a will or trust can be a specified dollar amount or a percentage of the estate. Since the final size of the estate is uncertain at the time the will is written, it is often more desirable to use percentages than dollar amounts to describe how the estate is to be distributed.

One of the benefits of a will or trust is that it can be changed at any time. A person can reevaluate his or her giving priorities as family and financial circumstances change over time. Any gift through a will or trust to a qualified charity is deductible for Federal Estate Tax purposes.

Life Estate Gift

A donor may deed a personal residence, farm, or other real property to the Lord's work now, but retain lifetime enjoyment and use of the property. The donor may continue to live in the home. In the case of other property, the donor may continue to collect any income generated. The donor continues to pay the taxes, insurance, and maintenance of the property.

At the donor's death, the property becomes the immediate property of the charity. It could then sell the property and use the cash proceeds. In the case of a personal residence, a church may decide to keep the home for use by pastoral staff or visiting missionaries, or ministry expansion.

An irrevocable Life Estate Gift will generate a tax-deductible gift based on the "remainder interest" the person holds in the property. This value is determined according to government tables and the donor's age. This amount may be claimed as a deduction for Federal Income Tax purposes in the year the agreement is completed. This arrangement removes the property from the estate, and it will not be subject to either probate or the Federal Estate Tax.

Life Insurance Gifts

Life insurance is one way of making a larger gift than a donor may be able to make otherwise. This gift option is available for both new and existing policies. If done properly, the annual premiums paid on the policy can be deducted as a charitable gift for Federal Income Tax purposes.

Life insurance proceeds are included in the gross estate for calculation of the Federal Estate Tax. If the beneficiary of the policy is a qualified charity, there is a charitable deduction for purposes of the Federal Estate Tax.

Charitable Remainder Unitrust

The Charitable Remainder Unitrust is designed for the donor who wants to make a gift to the Lord's work, but needs income during life. This trust is especially suited for a donor with highly appreciated property (either securities or real estate). It is possible to transfer the property to the trust and avoid all tax on capital gain.

A Federal Income Tax deduction is available for the year the trust is created. It is based on the value of the trust, the age of the donor, and the payout percentage selected. A Charitable Remainder Unitrust may be created and funded at the time of death for the benefit of one or more survivors. Assets transferred to the trust would not be subject to probate or the Federal Estate Tax.

One or more charitable beneficiaries may be named in the trust. At the death of the donors the assets from the trust would be distributed to these charities. The Charitable Remainder Unitrust is one of the most technical gift plans, and requires expert help to both set up and manage. A church's denominational foundation or independent counsel should be able to assist from the beginning to the end of this process.

Charitable Lead Trust

The Charitable Lead Trust is almost the opposite of the Charitable Remainder Unitrust. The donor creates a trust to provide current income to a charitable organization for a specified period of time (5, 10, 15, or more years). At the end of that time the assets of the trust are returned to family members. The Charitable Lead Trust may help wealthy families transfer assets to heirs, with little or no estate or gift tax. Seek professional counsel.

Gift Annuity Agreement/Deferred Gift Annuity Agreement

The Gift Annuity Agreement is a perfect plan for a donor who wants to make a future gift and receive a guaranteed stream of income for life. Annuity rates are based on age and are often quite competitive with what a donor can earn from low risk investments in the market. A deferred payment annuity allows for payments to begin at a later day (such as at retirement) and results in both a larger charitable gift and a greater annual income. Both immediate and deferred annuity plans are an excellent means of "supplementing" retirement income but are not meant to be retirement plans.

The Charitable Gift Annuity is less complicated than a Charitable Remainder Unitrust (CRUT), but the CRUT has greater flexibility and applications.

This plan provides a Federal Income Tax deduction in the year that the annuity is entered. The amount of the gift is determined by the age of the annuitant, the annuity rate, and the principal amount.

Another advantage of the gift annuity is that part of the annual income is considered tax-exempt. Also, if the annuity is funded with appreciated securities, there is significant savings related to capital gains tax. A portion of the capital gain is avoided altogether, and the remainder is reported in small increments over the life expectancy of the annuitant.

All remaining funds in the agreement at the annuitant's death are available for the ministries designated by the donor. The amount placed in the annuity during life is removed from the estate and will not be subject to probate or the Federal Estate Tax.

The Gift Annuity Agreement and Deferred Gift Annuity Agreement are less complicated than the Charitable Remainder Unitrust. However, few churches or smaller Para-church ministries would be able to administer their own annuity program. Again, refer to your denominational or independent counsel, or check with a local or national *Christian Foundation.* Several are listed at the end of this chapter. These foundations can provide assistance in placing a planned gift plus gift administration services.

Other Planned Gifting

1. *Living Trust.* The Living Trust is a good "will substitute" estate-planning tool for some families. Such a trust can be written to include a charitable bequest, just like in a will. Assets in the trust are distributed according to the terms of the trust and do not pass through the probate process.

2. *Naming the Church as Beneficiary.* One easy method of making a planned gift is by naming the church or non-profit organization as beneficiary of any account that allows such a designation. A checking account or savings account would be one example. In a banking situation this is often known as a Pay on Death (or POD) account. Some institutions may refer to this arrangement as Transfer on Death (or TOD). These arrangements allow for the assets to pass directly to the named beneficiary and avoid the probate process.

3. *Retirement Plans.* Retirement plans allow the owner to name a beneficiary, or beneficiaries. At the death of some high wealth individuals, there may be two taxes levied against a qualified or tax deferred retirement account— income and estate. These taxes can be avoided if the "secondary" beneficiary of the plan is a qualified charity. This is "win-win" because family members would end up inheriting the same amount or more when using this tax strategy. With married couples, when a spouse dies, the "primary" beneficiary is usually the other spouse. The surviving spouse could then "roll" the tax-deferred retirement account into a personal tax-deferred retirement account and continue to defer any income taxes. But when he or she dies and the proceeds of the account go to a "non-spouse," like children, that becomes a "taxable event."

Current tax law changes allow children to "stretch out" their receipt and subsequent taxation of the proceeds. However, by naming a charity as the "secondary" beneficiary, some or all of potential income taxes can be avoided. Since other assets in the estate may not be subject to income taxes at death, such as cash, life insurance or real estate, consider "using" the tax deferred retirement account for any charitable bequests and pass the other assets to children and friends.

4. *Automatic Transfers.* Automatic transfers at death are often referred to as "will substitutes" because they bypass distribution through the will. Such transfers avoid the probate process. These assets will avoid the Federal Estate Tax when transferred to a qualified charity. Examples are joint tenancy, life insurance, IRAs and business agreements.

5. *Endowments*. These funds can be set up so that members can make current or deferred gifts into the endowment, knowing that it will annually give from the earnings of the investment portfolio in the fund. It is a good way for the church or Para-church ministry to endorse the future of its own ministries, in particular giving to missions. It can produce an economic "hedge" against hard times. The danger to avoid is allowing the church to become dependent for its regular budget on the income from the endowment. For help in setting up an endowment, you can seek help from a local or national Christian Foundation.

6. *Outright Gifts (other than cash)*
Gifts other than cash can be a significant benefit to a local church or Para-church ministry, like a school. Such gifts might include stocks, bonds, mutual fund shares, real property, or tangible property. Non-cash gifts often require special handling, and at times the organization should say "no thanks" to certain gifts. Transfer of ownership will often require some form of legal document. There are special Internal Revenue Service (USA) rules for valuing

and reporting non-cash gifts. At any rate, your church should *set up a brokerage account* in order to receive any gifts of securities. The tax-deductible value of some gifts will be limited to the donor's cost basis or the Fair Market Value (which ever is lower). Donors will be allowed to deduct the full value of some gifts (including all appreciation), and will avoid any tax on capital gain. Any property given during life will be removed from the estate and will not be subject to probate or the Federal Estate Tax. There should be a *legal disclaimer* that any gift planning information provided to a donor by your organization is for educational purposes only. Every donor is entitled to independent legal counsel as he or she considers including charitable giving as part of his or her estate plan.

Promoting Planned Giving in Your Church or Organization

The most productive way is to conduct estate/gift planning seminars once or twice a year. Invite qualified estate-planning attorneys from your community, if any, to conduct seminars for your people. Provide literature on aspects of estate and gift-planning. You can obtain these from denominational offices as well as companies that serve this area of financial planning.

Promoting Bequests

1. Include a statement in your newsletter, church worship folder, or other organization communication piece that says something like this: "Have you considered naming [your organization name] in your will? Just as you tithe your income, you can tithe your estate. This way you can continue to support the ministries of [your organization name] after you are called 'home.' Call our office for more information on how to do this."
2. Include a "Will" brochure in your literature rack (available through your denomination or independent sources).

3. Offer educational opportunities to your people such as an estate-planning seminar. This is the **most effective way,** or "system," to generate planned gifts. It creates a "momentum" of interest and motivation toward implementing a family's estate and charitable plan. My experience in conducting many financial and estate planning seminars has demonstrated very productive results. I encourage you to use these seminars to encourage your people in the area of gift planning.
4. Include estate-planning information in your church, school or organization library.
5. If you have an attorney in your church or community who specializes in estate planning, ask him or her to make a presentation.
6. Make use of testimonials of how your church (or others you know about) have benefited by way of a special gift through a person's will.
7. Include testimonials of folks who have benefited from providing a planned gift, such as reduced taxes, more income, or the joy of helping their organization expand its ministry.
8. Personally visit potential planned giving donors in your church or organization. Have your Senior Pastor or top leadership accompany the qualified person who will be making the presentation. It may be a representative from your denomination's foundation or a professional consultant. This can be very effective as a follow-up consultation after a seminar.

Promoting a Life Estate Gift

Since you will need professional assistance for implementing this type of a deferred gift, you probably should not promote it directly. Just understand how this gift works and be ready to suggest it to the right person.

Promoting a Life Insurance Gift

- Some people have old life insurance policies they no longer need. They may be paid-up policies with significant cash value. Let your people know that they can gift those policies directly to the organization, who in turn can decide whether to cash them out or wait until it receives the death benefits.
- Another option is to encourage them to add your church or organization as one of the beneficiaries of an existing policy. Remind them to first determine if all of the settlement proceeds will be needed by their family. You don't want them to disinherit their family.
- You can also promote the concept of "tithing" their life insurance proceeds just like in their will or living trust. They do this by changing their beneficiary designations.
- All of this information can be presented in your newsletter, a worship folder insert, at an estate-planning seminar, a direct letter to your people, on your website, or in an announcement during a worship service.

Promoting a Charitable Remainder Unitrust (CRUT)

You can present a "teaser" like this in your newsletter or a special insert in your worship folder: *"Could you use more income? Do you have appreciated assets that are not generating much, if any income? Would you like to avoid capital gain tax on that appreciated asset? The good news is that you can accomplish all of this, and more and also make a significant future gift to the ministries of (name of your church or ministry). Call (name of individual) for more information."* You are looking for someone who has a desire to benefit the church or ministry, needs additional income and who has highly appreciated assets that generate little or no income. The *five key selling points* of the CRUT are:

- It allows you to avoid capital gains tax.
- It can increase your income.
- It gives you an income tax deduction.

- It reduces your potential estate tax.
- It allows you to make a future gift to God's kingdom.

Promoting a Charitable Lead Trust

The Charitable Lead Trust is rarely used and would most often be of interest to the very wealthy. If you have high-net-worth families in your church or organization, encourage them to seek the counsel of a Christian foundation, charitable organization's planned giving department, or an attorney that specializes in trusts and estate planning, and who is sympathetic to charitable giving.

Promoting a Gift Annuity Agreement

Many older people could use additional income, and Gift Annuity rates are often much higher than Certificate of Deposit rates. In your promotional material, say something like this: *"Could you use more income? Do you have Certificates of Deposits that are not generating that much income for you? Consider transferring some of it to a Gift Annuity Agreement. It can provide more income, some of it tax-free, reduce your income taxes and allow you to make a significant future gift to the ministries of (name of your church or ministry)."* This charitable vehicle would also apply to someone who would like to give more but is on a fixed income. (Reminder: The donor must give up control of the principal since it becomes an irrevocable transfer of assets into the Annuity Agreement.)

Promoting a Deferred Gift Annuity Agreement

For people who have "maxed" out their qualified retirement plans, such as a 401K or profit sharing plan, the deferred gift annuity might be of interest. They defer the income payout until a later time, such as retirement. Because of the potential build-up of principal until then, the future payout can have a higher than market "rate of return." The charity (your non-profit organization) sells the stock when its value is high, with no capital gain tax, and starts paying out the required income stream when the donor wants it. A seminar would be the best way to promote these ideas and advantages to your people. Be sure to refer them to proper counsel, such as your denominational office or the foundations mentioned at the end of this chapter.

Promoting Other Gifts

- Let God's people know that you are willing to accept non-cash gifts that meet your gift acceptance policies. This may be especially helpful during a capital improvement program. Examples of a non-cash gift would be vehicles, real estate, tangibles, building materials, professional services. You will need professional assistance in determining whether you should accept a real estate gift as well as making the transfer itself. You don't want to get stuck with real estate encumbered with environmental or title problems.
- Near the end of the calendar year, encourage people to evaluate their giving. This is a good time to remind people that a donation of stock might be a "tax wise" way to give. If their stock has appreciated, they should donate the stock and avoid capital gain tax. They will be able to deduct the current market value of the stock. If their stock has depreciated in value, they should sell the stock first, then gift the sale proceeds, taking the income tax deduction for the loss.

How to Generate and Administer Planned Gifts

Once you have uncovered a potential planned gift, use professional resources in your area to complete the gift. This could involve a planned giving representative from a charitable organization, consultant, estate planning attorney, financial planner, CPA, stock-broker, insurance agent and/or real estate agent. You will want to open a stock brokerage account for your organization in order to receive stock gifts. And, you will want to consider utilizing the services of a Christian foundation, such as the ones mentioned at the end of this chapter. Since few churches or non-profit ministries are large enough to warrant establishing their own foundation, these Christian foundations can allow even a small church or organization to benefit from a sophisticated planned gift.

Although the individual donor can function as the administrator of a planned gift, most donors would rather give that responsibility to a professional trust service. Some banks offer this service and there are companies that specialize in administering planned gifts. If your church is a part of a denomination, its foundation can possibly provide that service. Or use one of the independent Christian foundations mentioned at the end of this chapter. Administrating a planned gift involves the correct accounting and tax reporting of the trust disbursements and assets. It can be complicated.

Resources Available to Help With Your Estate and Gift Planning Program

- **Seminar Material**
  You should have an estate-planning attorney and/or financial planner present these types of seminars because of their technical requirements. *Kingdom Advisors* is an excellent source for qualified and certified financial and legal professionals who are equipped and trained to conduct financial, estate and gift planning seminars. You can learn more at www.kingdomadvisors.org. Be sure to provide for "free" follow-up consultation appointments for those attending. This is very important to motivate those attending to follow through and implement their necessary estate plan and avoid procrastination. This is especially true when presenting the idea of making a planned gift. This is a new concept to most people, and they will need the reinforcement of talking one-on-one with a professional who can explain it clearly to them. Those professionals being used to conduct the seminars can be the ones who provide the personal consultations.
- **Books and Literature**
  - "Gift of a Lifetime – Planned Giving in Congregational Life," by J. Gregory Pope, Broad-

man & Holman Publishers. The ISBN is 0-8054-1848-2. The author provides much detail including sample forms, letters, wills and trust documents, and a glossary of stewardship and planned giving terms.

- "Giving from the Heart- A Legacy That Lasts Forever" by Dan Busby, CPA. This is a booklet published by the *Evangelical Council for Financial Accountability (ECFA)*. The author covers some basic and biblical principles for giving, along with some examples of givers. He then gets into the legal and technical details of gifts to family and charities such as outright gifts, securities, real estate, life insurance and planned gifts such as charitable remainder unitrusts, gift annuities and giving from retirement accounts. You can provide copies for your donor prospects. You can reach them at 440 W Jubal Early Dr, Suite 130, Winchester, VA, 22601, 800-323-9473, or www.ecfa.org.

- Schumacher Publishing. Vickie and Jim Schumacher are authors and publishers of the book *Understanding Living Trusts*. They also publish personalized brochures for churches and organizations on different aspects of living trusts, estate tax law, charitable trusts and other advanced estate-planning strategies. You can order these materials by visiting their website at www.estateplanning.com.

- **Consultants**
  - **Crescendo Interactive**. This company provides software, educational seminars, multimedia and Internet service to organizations seeking to offer planned giving counsel to their people. They have a large client base of non-profits using their software. Their address is 110 Camino Ruiz, Camarillo, CA, 93012. Their phone number is (800) 858-9154; fax

is (805) 388-2483. You can e-mail them at crespro@cresmail.com. They have three websites: www.crescendointeractive.com (their main one), www.GiftLaw.com (a comprehensive source of planned giving law and information) and www.GiftLegacy.com (an interactive calculator program for donors to evaluate the mathematical options for making a particular gift). Once you install their software, you can produce presentation seminars using their PowerPoint slides.

- **PhilanthroCorp.** They are a fee-only, planned giving *outsource* company. They can help expand an existing planned giving program, or establish a new one. They can work directly with your potential donors, or train you to do it. Since most churches and smaller non-profit organizations do not have a planned giving capability, this company can "act" as their planned giving department if they do not have access to a denominational planned giving service. They also offer a web-based planned giving system for churches. That website is www.pcxhome.com. Their mailing address is P.O. Box 6190, Woodland Park, CO, 80866. Their phone number is (800) 876-7958 ext. 401.Their general website is www.plannedgift.com, and e-mail is dkeesling@plannedgift.com.

- **Foundations for Servicing Planned Gifts**
  - **The National Christian Foundation (NCF)** is the largest Christian grant-making foundation in the world. It allows churches, schools and Para-church ministries to direct planned gifts of their members to a "community" foundation that serves as trustee and administrator on behalf of the donor and charitable beneficiary of the current or deferred gift. It can issue "private label" gift annuities on behalf of the church or organization. Individuals can utilize

these services through their "Donor Advised Funds" (DAF). They name the DAF as the charitable beneficiary of their will, trust, annuity, retirement plan or insurance policy at the time of their death. During their lifetime they "advise" the foundation where to direct their funds. Their children can be listed to continue the legacy of the donor(s). Also a "charity advised fund" is offered where a church or organization can "advise" where gift funds to itself will go to selected ministries. The benefit of The National Christian Foundation is that it allows your church or non-profit to provide planned giving administrative services for your members without the high cost of setting up and running your own charitable foundation. They have multiple local offices and staff throughout the United States working with individual givers, their professional advisors, churches and ministries. Their National office address is 11625 Rainwater Drive, Suite 500, Alphareta, GA, 30009. Their phone numbers are (404) 252-0100 & (800) 681-6223. Fax # is (888) 672-7302. You can e-mail them at info@nationalchristian.com and their website is www.nationalchristian.com.

- **WaterStone.** This is also a national community foundation providing charitable giving services. It allows churches and non-profit organizations to direct planned gifts of their members to a "community" foundation that serves as trustee and administrator on behalf of the donor and charitable beneficiary of the current or deferred gift. It provides services similar to The National Christian Foundation. It also allows your church or non-profit to provide planned giving administrative services for your members without the high cost of setting up and running your own charitable foundation.

Their address is 2925 Professional Place, Suite 201, Colorado Springs, CO, 80904-8105. Their phone number is (719) 447-4620; fax is (719) 447-4700. You can reach them on their website www.waterstone.org.

- **Christian Foundation of the West.** CFW is designed with the same ideals in mind as the other two Christian foundations, that through giving we can help others. The Christian Foundation of the West works with individual givers, churches, ministries, and professional advisors in the area of charitable giving to transform our community for Christ. They provide the same type of services to donors and organizations as NCF and WaterStone. You can reach them at www.cfwest.com,

- **Administrative Services**
The administration of a charitable trust is a fairly challenging task. While an individual donor can undertake this responsibility with the advice of qualified counselors, there are several options:
    - **Corporate Trustees**, which includes banks, trust companies, and the trust departments of major financial firms.
    - **Charity as Trustee**, if they have that capability.
    - **Foundations**, if they provide that service.
    - **Private Trustee**, which can include the donor or independent companies, such as the following:
        - Premier Trust (888) 588-7878 www.premieradministration.com.
        - Renaissance Trust 800.479.5142 www.charitabletrust.com

CONCLUSION –

Think of these planned gifts as a "win-win" opportunity for donor, church, and/or charitable organization. Your organization should encourage its members to consider planned gifts. Proper motivation and adequate information can produce confident donors—and such donors will give greater resources for kingdom work and the glory of God. For most, it will be the largest gift they will ever make.

CHAPTER SIX –

CONCLUDING THOUGHTS

To review, stewardship & generosity *education* is at the core of a well-thought-out process of stewardship growth. Without long-term biblical stewardship & generosity education, other efforts at financial development and "fund-raising" will be limited and short-lived. As we have emphasized and hopefully you agree by now…

> *Stewardship is about more than money.*
> *It is a spiritual issue.*

As you prepare to plan and implement your comprehensive stewardship & generosity ministry, including possibly seeking professional help, here is a review of the list of *characteristics* of an effective stewardship and generosity ministry:
- It is rooted in sound biblical thinking.
- It is age-group specific and culturally appropriate.
- It addresses real life issues and meets people at their point of need.
- It focuses on developing Christian values and life principles.
- It encompasses a *total-life* view of stewardship & generosity, not just a seminar or bible study.
- It is done with excellence.
- It should be interesting and highly visual, drawing from multiple resources.
- It is a sustained and ongoing process. It will take several years.

My previous publication and Training Kit, *Resourcing Your Vision – A Church Stewardship Ministry Guide,* from which this book is taken, was designed to be a "do-it-yourself" publication just for churches. My experience, however, with client churches, and that of other similar stewardship and generosity ministry leaders, demonstrated that the vast majority of churches were unable to adequately and independently implement a tailored stewardship/generosity ministry without some professional counsel, support and accountability. There were **several reasons**:

- There was not strong enough support from the senior pastor, his staff, or lay board.
- The church was not able to recruit qualified lay leaders for the ministry team, thus ending up with weak team leadership.
- The senior pastor's attention was elsewhere. He/she didn't see this ministry as priority.
- The church leadership team and stewardship/generosity ministry leadership team were not held accountable and/or didn't follow the manual's training and instruction.

The bottom line is that you should seriously consider accepting some outside, professional help. Maybe you are the exception; but maybe you are not. Before you start your program, I encourage you at least, to call *VISION RESOURCING GROUP*, a non-profit ministry that is designed to provide this type of personal help. You can use them to help you determine *if* you need outside help.

In the interest of full disclosure, I am the Co-founder and President of Vision Resourcing Group, and Mr. Jim Sullivan is my Co-founder and Chief Executive Officer. He has over 20 years of leadership with Crown Financial Ministries. Between us we have over 40 years of experience in stewardship and generosity ministry training and implementation. Our passion all these years has been to see God's people become free financially, walk more intimately with the Lord Jesus, and grow in generosity. As a result, we want to see the church, His schools, and Para-church ministries to be fully resourced so that His people can fund the Great Commission, reaching the world for Christ. Following this introduction to

VISION RESOURCING GROUP, in Appendix One and Two I list a selection of **specific resources** you can access as you build your tailored stewardship/generosity ministry.

Working with other Partner stewardship & generosity teaching ministries, we provide resources that train and equip Christian Leaders to be more effective and successful in creating a culture of biblical stewardship and generosity in the lives of those people within their scope of influence." Said another way, we provide tailored training and guidance for Christian leaders to enable them to better develop a culture of biblical stewardship, leadership and generosity to their people. Our primary objective is to "train the trainer" through our consulting-equipping-supporting process. We meet with you to determine your goals and needs, help you develop a *tailored* action plan, equip you with selected resources, and follow up in supporting you toward success. We also *hold you accountable* to your committed goals so that your people prosper and you experience the joy of their growth.

To learn more, visit our website at www.visionresourcinggroup.com, or call our office at 949.916.7560, or e-mail us at info@visionresourcinggroup.com. You can also reach me, Dick Edic, at 619.579.8205 or dedic@visionresourcinggroup.com. There is no obligation, as we want to help you, and ourselves, determine **if** we want to work together. For those of you who are not located in Southern California, we can help you via conference calls, webinars, or one-on-one consultation. We are in the process of recruiting and training mature consultants in other areas who would be available to provide personalized and on-location training and assistance. We look forward to serving you.

APPENDIX ONE

Here are a few resources to help you get started. And, as a purchaser of this book, you are entitled to the free *additional resources* available on the Vision Resourcing Group website. Type in http://www.visionresourcinggroup.com/bookresources to access these *Free Resources"*. You will be asked to give some information about yourself, and setup your User Name and Password to gain instant access to these valuable resources. You can also scan this QR code with your Smart Phone which takes you directly to the *"Free Resources"* page.

Again, some or all of these resources listed below can be utilized within the basic leadership categories, Church, Para-Church, Business, School.

THEMES

So, what **THEMES** should you teach? Which ones are priority? God's Word teaches us principles on *every aspect* of stewardship and generosity, not just "giving" or "tithing". As I have studied and taught the subject, I have observed certain themes that I believe should be *basic* and *fundamental*. Certainly "giving" is one of them, but in order to fully appreciate and apply this important aspect of stewardship, we need to understand and embrace other *basic* and *fundamental* truths. Here is a brief overview, with selected Scriptures, of stewardship education ***themes*** to teach:

1. **God's part**
   - God owns it all—Psalm 50:10; 24:1; Haggai 2:8; 1 Chronicles 29:11-12; Leviticus 25:23
   - God is Lord of all—Genesis 1:1; Job 42:2; Psalm 135:6; Acts 17:26; Colossians 2:15
   - He is the provider of all—Psalm 16:5-6; Matthew 6:25-32; Ephesians 1:3; Philippians 4:19

2. **Man's part**
   - We are stewards—Genesis 1:26; Psalm 8:4-6; Leviticus 25:23; Hebrews 11:13
   - We are to be faithful—1 Corinthians 4:2; Luke 16:10-12; "Small things are small things, but faithfulness with a small thing is a big thing" (Hudson Taylor); Matthew 25:23
   - We are held accountable—Luke 12:48; Romans 14:12; 2 Corinthians 5:10

3. **Managing our time and talent**
   - God created our time and place on earth—Acts 17:26; Luke 12:19-20
   - God created our talent and spiritual gifts—Ephesians 2:10; 1 Peter 4:10-11; 1 Corinthians 12:1-11; Romans 12:6-8

4. **Don't waste time**—Ephesians 5:15-17; Psalm 90:12; Ecclesiastes 3:1
   - Work with all your heart for the Lord—Colossians 3:23-24
   - Don't presume on your future—James 4:13-15
   - Be diligent in all that you do—Proverbs 22:29; 27:23

- Don't forget to rest—Exodus 20:9-10

5. **Managing our money**
    - Don't love money—1 Timothy 6:10; Ecclesiastes 5:10
    - Be content with what you have—1 Timothy 6:6-8; Philippians 4:11-13; Hebrews 13:5
    - Don't live beyond your means—Proverbs 21:17
    - Be sure to save and invest—Proverbs 21:5, 20; 30:24-25; Genesis 41:34-36
    - Don't cosign notes—Proverbs 17:18; 22:26-27
    - Don't over-use credit cards—Proverbs 27:12
    - Set financial goals—Proverbs 16:9 LB; 24:2-4
    - Have an up-to-date estate plan—2 Kings 20:1
    - Establish and work a budget—Proverbs 27:23-24
    - Be willing to seek financial counsel—Proverbs 12:15
    - Avoid debt—Romans 13:8; Proverbs 22:7
    - Pay your debts—Psalm 37:21; Proverbs 3:27-28

6. **Giving our money**
    - Why Give? – 1 Chronicles 29:11-14; Proverbs 3:9-10; 2 Corinthians 8:7 etc. (See Lesson 10 of my teaching outline later, "Managing Your Resources God's Way")
    - More blessed to give—Acts 20:35; Luke 6:38
    - Let love motivate your giving—1 Corinthians 13:3
    - Give cheerfully—2 Corinthians 9:7; 8:2-3; Acts 4:32-36
    - Give systematically—1 Corinthians 16:2
    - Give proportionately—2 Corinthians 8:12-13
    - Give sacrificially—Hebrews 13:16
    - Give first to God before yourself—Proverbs 3:9
    - Give ten percent—Malachi 3:10; 2 Corinthians 9:6
    - "You can give without loving, but you cannot love without giving."

7. **Training your children**—Proverbs 22:6; Deuteronomy 6:6-7;11:18-19; Ephesians 6:4
8. **Pay your taxes**—Matthew 22:17-21; Romans 13:1-7
9. **Estate Planning**—2 Kings 20:1

More **theme content** can be found in some of the books listed below as well as the listed websites. This, along with a study of the listed biblical passages, will prepare you for successful teaching of the different stewardship themes.

> *FACT: To successfully penetrate the hearts of your people, you must repeatedly teach all the stewardship themes from every ministry platform you can.*

SERMONS

SERMON OUTLINES to help your pastor get started. He/she can modify them as he/she wishes. Other sample sermons on stewardship are available on www.generousgiving.org.

Sermon One: *Stewardship of Time—A Realistic Time Saver for Reliable Time Management*[11]
1. **Hindrances in Time Management**
   - *Time is a unique resource.* Time cannot be saved or kept as other items. We cannot rent, hire, buy or otherwise obtain it. We can only use time. If we don't use time, it is lost forever, since it can neither be recovered nor recycled. The supply of time is totally inelastic. The quantity never increases. We can't store it or recall it at will. Therefore, time is always scarce. Time is also irreplaceable, so we must treat it as precious since everything we do requires it. Many of us never realize the value of

---

[11] Alton Loveless, former general director of Randall House Publications, Nashville, TN. Used by permission.

this one unique resource God gives us to do His work. Of all the resources God gives us, time is probably the one of which we are the worst stewards. Since each of us has the same amount of time, the success and failure of our stewardship of time depend on how we use it.

- *Two types of Time*. Controllable and uncontrollable. Controllable time is time we schedule and plan for its use. Uncontrolled time is that other time segment over which we have no control, such as meetings or events we may be forced to attend. Being a caretaker of time takes practice.
- *Learn to log your time.*
- *Learn how to organize time. Learn how to set goals*. A time robber is any activity that hinders us from achieving things we should be doing or have planned to do.
- *Learn how effective people conserve time.*

2. **Aids in Time Management**.
- *Prepare a form or method to retrieve your lost time*, i.e., *what I plan to do tomorrow and what I did.*
- *Short and long-range plans begin with a measuring instrument*. List, prioritize, select the most important activity to do first, then evaluate mid-week, assign tasks to others, and conduct a follow-up evaluation of the week's activities.
- *Common schedule-breakers*. Can't say "no"; lack of commitment to managing your time; procrastination.

Sermon Two: *Three Types of Giving in the New Testament*[12]
1. **Systematic Giving** (1 Corinthians 16:1-3)
   - Giving should be weekly.
   - Giving is an individual responsibility.
   - Giving should be proportional.
2. **Spontaneous Giving** (2 Corinthians 9:6-8)
   - The principle (v.6)
   - The purpose (v.7)
   - The provision (v.8)
3. **Sacrificial Giving** (2 Corinthians 8:1-8)
   - It begins in self-surrender.
   - It begins out of poverty.

Sermon Three & Four: Brian Kluth, former pastor and past president of Christian Stewardship Association, author and speaker on generous living, printed these next two messages in their *Stewardship Resource Manual* (out of print; used by permission). His website, www.kluth.org has other sermon material on generosity. He says the following in the introduction of the first one, "In stewardship speaking engagements across America and on five continents, I have discovered two things:

- Christians of all income levels have experienced spiritual joy, supernatural grace, and divine help through the practice of making a specific commitment to GIVE 10% OR MORE of their resources to the Lord's work.
- The vast majority of pastors are reluctant to teach their congregations about money matters and Christian giving."

This list of 10 reasons to GIVE 10% OR MORE to the Lord's work was written to encourage laity and clergy that this subject can

---

[12] Leroy B. Lowery, *Together Way* manual, published by Randall House, rights owned by National Association of Freewill Baptists, Inc. Used by permission.

be biblically and practically taught and caught! When believers are taught to make it a priority to give to God first, it will ultimately bring greater financial freedom and blessing into their personal lives and to the ministries they support. Here are the messages:

Sermon Three – **"10 Biblical and Practical Reasons to give 10% or more of your income to the Lord's work":**

1. It is a tried and proven pattern of giving done by godly people throughout the ages, regardless of cultures and income levels. (Genesis 14:17-20; 28:16-22; Leviticus 27:30; Proverbs 3:9-10; Malachi 3:7-15; Matthew 23:23)
2. It will help you revere God more in your life. (Deuteronomy 14:23)
3. It will bring God's wisdom and order to your finances and will help you harness the dragon of materialism. (Matthew 6:19-21, 24-34; Luke 12:16-21; 1 Timothy 6:6-10,17-19; Ecclesiastes 5:10)
4. It will serve as a practical reminder that God is the owner of everything you have. (1 Chronicles 29:11-18; Psalm 24:1-2; 50:10-12; Haggai 2:8)
5. It will allow you to experience God's creative care and provisions in ways that you would not otherwise experience. (1 Kings 17; Proverbs 3:9,10; Malachi 3:7-15; Haggai 1:4-11; 2:15-19; Luke 6:38; Deuteronomy 28; Phil. 4:15-19; Mark 12:41-44)
6. It will encourage your spiritual growth and trust in God. (Deuteronomy 14:23; Proverbs 3:5-6; Malachi 3:8-10; Haggai 1:4-11; 2:15-19; 2 Corinthians 8:5)
7. It will ensure you of treasure in heaven. (1 Timothy 6:18-19; Matthew 6:19-21; Hebrews 6:10; 3 John 8; 1 Samuel 30:22)
8. It will strengthen the ministry, outreach and stability of your local church. (Acts 2:42-47; 4:32; 2 Corinthians 9:12-13)
9. It will help provide the means to keep your pastor and missionaries in full-time Christian service. (1 Corinthians

9:9-11,14; 1 Timothy 5:17-18; 3 John 5-8; Philippians 4:15-19; Galatians 6:6; Luke 8:3; 2 Kings 4:8-10)
10. It will help accomplish needed building projects and renovations. (2 Chronicles 24:4-14; Exodus 35, 36; 2 Kings 12:2-16; 1 Chronicles 29:2-19; Ezekiel 1:4-6.)

NOTE: More sermons are on the Vision Resourcing Group website,. Type in http://www.visionresourcinggroup.com/bookresources *to access these "Free Resources". You will be asked to setup your User Name and Password to gain instant access to these valuable resources. You can also scan the QR code posted on the first page of Appendix One with your Smart Phone which takes you directly to the "Free Resources" page.*

SUNDAY SCHOOL OR CHRISTIAN EDUCATION TEACHING OUTLINES

These teaching outlines will help you teach stewardship and generosity to your adult Sunday school or Christian education classes. You can also adapt them to your high school and college-level classes, along with a business employee or school environment.

Before listing these teaching outlines, let's review some basic *principles* in teaching stewardship, and in particular, "giving":
1. Use the Bible!
2. Be positive. Teach the growth, blessings, vision and changed lives that come from biblical giving. Don't use criticism and threats of judgment.
3. Don't be apologetic about teaching stewardship. It is a part of discipleship.
4. Be honest. Don't make false promises about immediate riches coming from giving.

5. Teach "Faith-Sacrifice-Investment," rather than "Faith-Promise-Giving." God desires sacrifice more than promises.

   Faith is required because we cannot physically see God's provision and the results of our giving at the time we give. We must trust God.

   Sacrifice is required because we must give up something in order to give to God, like more "stuff," or more "recreation."

   Investment is a better term than "giving" (although "giving" is OK) because God throughout eternity will return to us in proportion to our sacrifice more than we have given. It is also an investment in people who will be saved and changed for eternity. A worthy God deserves a worthy sacrifice for a worthy cause.

6. Help people identify what they will give up in order to be able to increase their investment in the things of God. This will help them appreciate the greater value of the "things of God" in comparison to those "things they will give up."

7. Communicate the cause and effect relationship between giving and the fulfillment of the vision of your church.

NOTE: More teaching outlines are on the Vision Resourcing Group website. Type in http://www.visionresourcinggroup.com/bookresources to access these *"Free Resources". You will be asked to setup your User Name and Password to gain instant access to these valuable resources. You can also scan the QR code posted on the first page of Appendix One with your Smart Phone which takes you directly to the "Free Resources" page. The first free teaching outline provided on our website is my "Managing Your Resources God's Way" – Ten Lessons. To whet your appetite, here are the 10 topics:*

1. What Is God's Part?
2. What Is Our Part?
3. Time and Talent

4. Managing Our Money: Principles and Mistakes
5. Saving and Investing
6. Teaching Children About Finances
7. How Much Is Enough?
8. Contentment
9. Attitudes in Giving of Our Resources
10. Benefits and Reasons for Giving

Outline #1 - Seven Principles of Stewardship That Provide the Framework for a Christian Lifestyle of Stewardship (A <u>Teaching Outline</u> taken from the Executive Summary, *Stewardship and the Kingdom of God,* Christian & Missionary Alliance Church; used with permission)

1. **Good stewardship begins with the recognition that God is the owner of all things.** (1 Chronicles 29:1-4; Luke 12:42-48; 16:1-13; 19:12-27; Matthew 25:14-20) We cannot "give" God ownership of our material goods. He already owns it all. We can only recognize and submit to His ownership.

2. **As stewards, we are entrusted with goods to care for as part of kingdom discipleship until the return of the Master Jesus Christ.** (Matthew 25:15, 27; Luke 19:23; 12:42) God is mainly concerned about our faithfulness with what He entrusts to our care. We can trust that God in His providence puts into our hands only what we can aptly handle and that He expects us to bear fruit in His kingdom.

3. **Earthly resources can be used for eternal purposes.** (Luke 16:13-15; Hebrews 6:10) Worldly wealth can have eternal value. We are to view money as a tool that can accomplish eternal work—-reaching people for Christ.

4. **Our stewardship must serve not only our own purposes, but the purpose of the Master, Jesus Christ.** (Luke 12:47; 17:7-10) The greatest punishment in the parable of the faithful and unfaithful servants comes to the servant who knew the master's will and did not do it.

5. **As stewards we need a balanced picture of hardship.** (Matthew 8:19-22; 10:22; Mark 10:45) God has often called his people to endure hardship, but a balanced view is necessary. We should resist lifestyle inflation to minimize debt, increase giving, and be ready to support God's call to new ministry.
6. **We will be held accountable for our stewardship.** (2 Corinthians 5:10; Ephesians 2:8-9; Matthew 16:27; 1 Corinthians 3:10-15; Romans 14:12) Our redemption does not remove us from responsibility and accountability before God. It will be an evaluation of both deed and heart.
7. **Our stewardship embraces both the spiritual and the material.** (Ephesians 5:15-16; 1 Corinthians 6:19; Hebrews 13:2; 1 Peter 4:9) The use of time and opportunities to minister certainly must be governed with wise stewardship.

Outline #2 - Tithing, Giving and Consumerism (Three lessons by Dr. Michael Reeves, President of the United Methodist Foundation of Louisiana; used with permission.)
1. **Tithing.** There are many references to the issue of tithing in the Bible. In the Old Testament tithing can be found in Leviticus 27:30-32; Deuteronomy 12:5-19 and again in Deuteronomy 14:28-29 and 26:12-15. In the New Testament there are four references, including Matthew 23:23; Luke 11:42 and 18:12; Hebrews 7:4-9.
   Read Malachi 3:6-11 and answer the following questions:
   - How can the people of God be blessed by God?
   - What is involved in returning to the Lord? How does God return?
   - When have you ever put God to this kind of test? What has happened?
   - According to most researchers, only about 5% of church members today tithe. Is the tithe still relevant today?
   - Is the tithe relevant in all cultures and situations?

- The Malachi passage mentions the "storehouse" in verse 10; what is the "storehouse" today? (*Answer*: the church.)
- What is the relevance of this passage for you? For your ministry?

2. **Giving**

   Read 2 Corinthians 8:1-15; 9:1-15 and answer the following questions:

   - Who is speaking to whom?
   - What do we know about Paul, the Corinthians' leaders, and the church in Macedonia?
   - According to verse 5, what is the motivation of giving?
   - Why should commands to give be unnecessary?
   - How has your giving supplied others?
   - How has someone's giving to you supplied you?
   - Find the principles of giving in Chapter 9 and paraphrase them.
   - What principles in Chapter 9 could improve your approach to giving?
   - In what way are these principles in Chapter 9 presently a reality in your daily experience?

3. **Consumerism.** John Wesley preached his great stewardship sermon, "The Use of Money," in which he said that we should "Gain all we can, Save all we can, and Give all we can." Today we seem to **gain** all we can, so we can **keep** all we can, so we can **spend** all we can. In the United States, our culture is very consumer-oriented, with the average teenager and adult hearing hundreds of appealing commercial messages each week.

   Read Matthew 6:19-34 and answer the following questions:

   - How do Christians counter the dominant cultural value of self-indulgence? Are the treasures of heaven and earth mutually exclusive?

- Contrast the characteristics of two masters. Which one would you rather serve?
- What things have made you anxious this past week?
- Who benefits from anxiousness? Who is hurt? Why?
- What are the ultimate goals in your life? How do your daily activities relate to them? To what extent?
- As you reflect on these three Bible studies, what will you do differently in the future? What have you learned from these studies?

COPY FOR "STEWARDSHIP MOMENTS"

Worship Services provide an opportunity to teach stewardship through regular "stewardship moments" just before you take the offering. Take one or two minutes to have someone share a brief testimony of how he or she has benefited from stewardship growth, such as tithing or getting out of credit card debt. Be sure to review with them what they are going to say and emphasize the importance of keeping it to one or two minutes. You can also have someone from your stewardship leadership team **read a verse or quote** on some aspect of stewardship. People need to be reminded, even if for a brief moment, of their stewardship responsibility and opportunity. One of your leadership team will need to be assigned the responsibility of coordinating this with your church worship team. In addition to these selected texts, you will find some quotes and additional verses in "Quotes, Factoids, Verses, Miscellaneous" below. Obviously, this material can be used in other settings besides church worship services.

When introducing this "stewardship moment" in your worship service, here is a *suggested statement*: "Before we take the offering, _____(name)_____ , from our stewardship leadership team, will share a stewardship thought." The introduced stewardship leadership team member can then say, "Hear what God says" (if reading a verse); "Hear what _____says" (name

159

author of a quote); "_____ will share a testimony" (Introduce the person giving their stewardship or giving testimony). Have the individual sharing their testimony write it out and then read it in order to avoid having them wander for two long. Another way to control it is to video tape it and show that rather than having them speak live to the congregation. It also will help avoid them becoming intimidated having to speak directly to the congregation.

Here is a list of suggested verse texts for 52 weeks:
1. "So if you have not been trustworthy in handling worldly wealth, who will trust you with true riches?" (Luke 16:11).
2. "Yours, O Lord, is the greatness and the power and the glory and the majesty and the splendor, for everything in heaven and earth is your. Yours, O Lord, is the kingdom. You are exalted as head over all. Wealth and honor come from you; you are the ruler of all things. In your hands are strength and power to exalt and give strength to all" (1 Chronicles 29:11-12).
3. "The earth is the Lord's, and everything in it, the world, and all who live in it" (Psalm 24:1).
4. "Now it is required that those who have been given a trust must prove faithful" (1 Corinthians 4:2).
5. "Honor the Lord with your wealth, with the first fruits of all your crops; then your barns will be filled to overflowing, and your vats will brim over with new wine" (Proverbs 3:9-10).
6. "The blessing of the Lord brings wealth, and he adds no trouble to it" (Proverbs 10:22).
7. "Ascribe to the Lord, O families of nations, ascribe to the Lord glory and strength, ascribe to the Lord the glory due his name. Bring an offering and come before him; worship the Lord in the splendor of his holiness" (1 Chronicles16:28-29).
8. "…remembering the words the Lord Jesus Himself said, 'It is more blessed to give than to receive'"(Acts 20:35).
9. "For you know the grace of our Lord Jesus Christ, that though He was rich, yet for your sakes He became poor, so that

through His poverty we might become rich" (2 Corinthians 8:9).

10. Moses said to the whole Israelite community, "This is what the Lord has commanded: Take from what you have, an offering for the Lord. Everyone who is willing is to bring to the Lord an offering..." (Exodus 35:4-5).

11. "But seek first His kingdom and His righteousness, and all these things will be given you as well" (Matthew 6:33).

12. "The rich rule over the poor, and the borrower is servant to the lender" (Proverbs 22:7).

13. "In the house of the wise are stores of choice food and oil, but a foolish man devours all he has" (Proverbs 21:20).

14. "Give, and it will be given to you. A good measure, pressed down, shaken together and running over, will be poured into your lap. For with the measure you use, it will be measured to you" (Luke 6:38).

15. "Do not store up for yourselves treasures on earth, where moth and rust destroy, and where thieves break in and steal. But store up for yourselves treasures in heaven, where moth and rust do not destroy, and where thieves do not break in and steal. For where your treasure is, there your heart will be also" (Matthew 6:19-21).

16. "Through Jesus, therefore, let us continually offer to God a sacrifice of praise—the fruit of lips that confess His name. And do not forget to do good and to share with others, for with such sacrifices God is pleased" (Hebrews 13:15-16).

17. "Remember this: Whoever sows sparingly will also reap sparingly, and whoever sows generously will also reap generously. Each man should give what he has decided in his heart to give, not reluctantly or under compulsion, for God loves a cheerful giver" (2 Corinthians 9:6-7).

18. "A generous man will himself be blessed, for he shares his food with the poor" (Proverbs 22:9).

19. "Each of you must bring a gift in proportion to the way the Lord your God has blessed you" (Deuteronomy 16:17).

20. "Keep your lives free from the love of money and be content with what you have, because God has said, "'Never will I leave you; never will I forsake you.'" (Hebews 13:5)
21. "The plans of the diligent lead to profit as surely as haste leads to poverty" (Proverbs 21:5).
22. "On the first day of every week, each one of you should set aside a sum of money in keeping with his income, saving it up, so that when I come no collections will have to be made" (1 Corinthians 16:1).
23. "…If you spend yourselves in behalf of the hungry and satisfy the need of the oppressed, then your light will rise in the darkness, and your night will become like noonday" (Isaiah 58:10).
24. "But just as you excel in everything—in faith, in speech, in knowledge, in complete earnestness and in your love for us— see that you also excel in this grace of giving" (2 Corinthians 8:7).
25. "Ascribe to the Lord the glory due His name; bring an offering and come into His courts. Worship the Lord in the splendor of His holiness; tremble before Him, all the earth" (Psalm 96:8-9).
26. "Now He who supplies seed to the sower and bread for food will also supply and increase your store of seed and will enlarge the harvest of your righteousness. You will be made rich in every way so that you can be generous on every occasion, and through us your generosity will result in thanksgiving to God" (2 Corinthians 9:10-11).
27. "Do not be deceived: God cannot be mocked. A man reaps what he sows" (Galatians 6:7).
28. "What good is it for a man to gain the whole world, yet forfeit his soul?" (Mark 8:36).
29. "No one can serve two masters. Either he will hate the one and love the other, or he will be devoted to the one and despise the other. You cannot serve both God and Money" (Matthew 6:24).

30. "...for I have learned to be content whatever the circumstances. I know what it is to have plenty. I have learned the secret of being content in any and every situation, whether well fed or hungry, whether living in plenty or in want. I can do everything through Him who gives me strength" (Philippians 4:11-13).

31. "But godliness with contentment is great gain. For we brought nothing into the world, and we can take nothing out of it. But if we have food and clothing, we will be content with that" (1 Timothy 6:6-8).

32. "People who want to get rich fall into temptation and a trap and into many foolish and harmful desires that plunge men into ruin and destruction. For the love of money is a root of all kinds of evil. Some people, eager for money, have wandered from the faith and pierced themselves with many griefs" (1 Timothy 6:9-10).

33. "He who gives to the poor will lack nothing, but he who closes his eyes to them receives many curses" (Proverbs 28:27).

34. "Command those who are rich in this present world not to be arrogant nor to put their hope in wealth, which is so uncertain, but to put their hope in God, who richly provides us with everything for our enjoyment" (1 Timothy 6:17).

35. "Command them (rich Christians) to do good, to be rich in good deeds, and to be generous and willing to share. In this way they will lay up treasure for themselves as a firm foundation for the coming age, so that they may take hold of the life that is truly life" (1 Timothy 6:18-19).

36. "Then He said to them, 'Watch out! Be on your guard against all kinds of greed; a man's life does not consist in the abundance of his possessions'" (Luke 12:15).

37. "The ground of a certain rich man produced a good crop. He thought to himself, 'What shall I do? I have no place to store my crops.' Then he said, 'This is what I will do. I will tear down my barns and build bigger ones, and there I will store all my grain and my goods. And I'll say to myself, "You have plenty of good things laid up for many years. Take life easy;

eat, drink and be merry.'" But God said to him, 'You fool! This very night your life will be demanded from you. Then who will get what you have prepared for yourself?' This is how it will be with anyone who stores up things for himself but is not rich toward God" (Luke 12:16-21).

38. "Each one should use whatever gift he has received to serve others, faithfully administering God's grace in its various forms" (1 Peter 4:10).

39. "...From everyone who has been given much, much more will demanded; and from the one who has been entrusted with much, much more will be asked" (Luke 12:48).

40. "Let no debt remain outstanding, except the continuing debt to love one another, for he who loves his fellowman has fulfilled the law" (Romans 13:8).

41. "But remember the Lord your God, for it is He who gives you the ability to produce wealth, and so confirms His covenant, which He swore to your forefathers, as it is today" (Deuteronomy 8:18).

42. "And now, brothers, we want you to know about the grace that God has given the Macedonian churches. Out of the most severe trial, their overflowing joy and their extreme poverty welled up in rich generosity. For I testify that they gave as much as they were able, and even beyond their ability. Entirely on their own, they urgently pleaded with us for the privilege of sharing in this service to the saints" (2 Corinthians 8:1-4).

43. "Every good and perfect gift is from above, coming down from the Father of the heavenly lights, who does not change like shifting shadows" (James 1:17).

44. "Now, our God, we give you thanks, and praise your glorious name. But who am I, and who are my people, that we should be able to give as generously as this? Everything comes from you, and we have given you only what comes from your hand" (1 Chronicles 29:13-14).

45. "All the believers were together and had everything in common. Selling their possessions and goods, they gave to anyone as he had need" (Acts 2:44).

46. "All the believers were one in heart and mind. No one claimed that any of his possessions was his own, but they shared everything they had" (Acts 4:32).

47. "There were no needy persons among them. For from time to time those who owned lands or houses sold them, brought the money from the sales and put it at the apostles' feet, and it was distributed to anyone as he had need" (Acts 4:34-35).

48. "Whoever trusts in his riches will fall, but the righteous will thrive like a green leaf" (Proverbs 11:28).

49. "One man gives freely, yet gains even more; another withholds unduly, but comes to poverty. A generous man will prosper; he who refreshes others will himself be refreshed" (Proverbs 11:24-25).

50. "Will a man rob God? Yet you rob me. But you ask, 'How do we rob you?' In tithes and offerings. You are under a curse— the whole nation of you—because you are robbing me" (Malachi 3:8-9).

51. "Bring the whole tithe into the storehouse, that there may be food in my house. Test me in this," says the Lord Almighty, "and see if I will not throw open the floodgates of heaven and pour out so much blessing that you will not have room enough for it" (Malachi 3:10).

52. So then, each of us will give an account of himself to God" (Romans 14:12).

NOTE: More verses are on the Vision Resourcing Group website. Type in http://www.visionresourcinggroup.com/bookresources *to access these "Free Resources". You will be asked to setup your User Name and Password to gain instant access to these valuable resources. You can also scan the QR code posted on the first page of Appendix One with your Smart Phone which takes you directly to the "Free Resources" page.*

Here are some other verses on giving that you can use...
Old Testament
Genesis 14:20; 28:20-22

Exodus 25:1-2; 35:20; 36:6-7
Leviticus 27:30
Deuteronomy 14:22-23
1 Kings 17:7-16
2 Corinthians 9:13; 8:12
Psalm 54:6
Proverbs 3:27-28; 14:21; 19:17; 21:13; 22:9; 25:14;
Haggai 1:4-11

New Testament
Matthew 10:42; 23:23; 25:35-36
Acts 10:4
Ephesians 5:1-2
Hebrews 6:10; 7:1-10
James 4:1-3; 1 John 3:17-18

COPY FOR NEWSLETTERS

As mentioned before, we live in an information "overloaded" culture. This challenge to your church or organization must be met with an aggressive strategy to communicate biblical stewardship and generosity to Christians. Repetition, repetition, repetition is the name of the game. And it must come from many sources, such as the printed page. The newsletter, electronic or hard-copy, is certainly one of those sources. Here are a few samples to get you started. More copy is available on the various websites mentioned in this book, such as www.generouschurch.com and generousgiving.org. You can use this "copy" section to create a stewardship column or section in your newsletter. You could title the column "T3" for time, talent and treasure. They could also be put in the form of a handout during your worship services, Sunday school classes, or put in the form of a letter to your people. Be creative. It will take time and effort to penetrate the minds and hearts of your congregation that are already filled with the world's perspective of time, talent and treasure. But, *be persistent*. Over time, utilizing all the "sources" available to you, including a lot of prayer, God will reward your efforts with changed lives and stronger stewardship and giving in your people.

Copy 1—Charles Swindoll gives the following illustration[13]—"I have been thinking about why the Scriptures teach 'It is more blessed to give than receive'" *Why is it that giving is preferred to receiving?* Here are a few reasons he gives:

- Giving encourages unselfishness within us.
- Giving brings others needed relief and encouragement.
- Giving forces us out of our own tight-radius world.
- Giving keeps us from becoming too attached to material things.
- Giving models the life Christ lived.
- Giving results in eternal rewards.
- Giving teaches us the value of servanthood.
- Giving makes us more cheerful, caring people.
- Giving prompts greater sensitivity toward others.
- Giving provides an example for others to follow.

No wonder the apostle Paul wrote that "God loves a cheerful giver." (2 Corinthians 9:7b)

Copy 2—Someone told of a good farmer who loved the Lord and believed in stewardship. He was very generous, and his friends asked why he gave so much and yet remained so prosperous.

"We cannot understand you," his friends said. "Why, you seem to give more than the rest of us, yet you seem to always have greater prosperity."

"Oh," the farmer replied, "that is very easy to explain. You see, I keep shoveling into God's bin, God keeps shoveling more and more into mine, and God has the bigger shovel!" (Note: this is a

---

[13] Charles Swindoll, *Insight for Living Letter,* January, 1991.

167

humorous story, but we need to remember that God's "shovel" my contain blessings *other* than money)

Copy 3 to 8 —Why Should We Give? (With the following introduction)

You can split this material into a separate part for each "reason," or combine some, depending on how much space you have available in your newsletter. If you place only one "reason" in each subsequent edition of your newsletter, add the heading *"Why Should We Give – Reason #_____."* Here is your introduction followed by the numbered reasons:

"Most of us want to mature in our faith in Christ. Possibly our prayer is the same as the apostle Paul's in Colossians 3:12, 'Not that I have already…been made perfect (mature), but I *press on* to take hold of that for which Christ Jesus took hold of me.'

For many of us, one of the most difficult areas to mature is in the area of giving, specifically *money*. The reasons are multiple, such as selfishness, insecurity, lack of trust in God's provision. We may have asked the question, *"Why does God want us to give?"* He already owns it all anyway, so why does He want our money?" Well, here are some *reasons,* with supporting scripture, to give:

1. Giving is part of God's *character*—It is His nature. He "...gives generously to all" and "richly provides us with everything for our enjoyment" (James 1:5; 1 Timothy 6:17). We are created in God's image. He has put His Spirit and nature in us. And as Christians, we have the mind of Christ (1 Corinthians 2:16). Our willingness to give is evidence of Christ's mind in us. God expresses His giving nature through us.

    Question: Are you letting God express this part of His nature through you...totally?

2. Giving *"proves"* our faith and love toward God (James 2:15-17; 1 John 3:17-18; 2 Corinthians 8:24)

    Question: How strong is your *proof*?

3. Giving is an act of *worship*. Giving merely to a church, a ministry or some needy person is only charity. Even though these entities need our giving, God wants us first to give to Him as an expression of our gratefulness and love for Him. In fact, in 2 Corinthians 9:7, when Paul talks about giving "cheerfully," the original Greek word means "hilarious."

   Question: Are you worshipping God through your giving with the same "exuberance" with which you sing and praise Him at Sunday morning worship services?

4. Giving *honors* God. "Honor the Lord with your wealth, with the first fruits of all your crops" (Proverbs 3:9-10). God knows that one of the greatest competitors to our love for Him is money. Therefore, He wants us to show our love for Him first! "For where your treasure is there your heart (honor) will be also...No one can serve (honor) two masters. Either he will hate the one and love the other, or he will be devoted to the one and despise the other. You cannot serve (honor) both God and money" (Matthew 6:21,24).

   Question: Are you honoring Him from *all* of your finances (before tax withholding), time and talent?

5. It reveals our *obedience* to Him. "Bring the whole tithe into the storehouse...."Command them to...be generous and willing to share" (Malachi 3:10; 1 Timothy 6:18). Jesus said in John 14:21 that our obedience to His commands proves our love for Him:

   Question: Are you more obedient in other areas of your Christian walk than in giving?

6. It shows our *maturity* in Christ. Paul told the Corinthians, "But just as you *excel* in everything—faith, in speech, in knowledge, in complete earnestness...see that you also excel in this grace of giving" (2 Corinthians 8:7).

   Question: How mature are you in giving?

7. It allows us to *give more*. Paul tells the Corinthians, "...and God is able to make all grace abound to you, so that in all things at all times, having all that you need, you will

abound in every good work...Now He who supplies seed to the sower and bread for food will also supply and *increase* your store of seed and will *enlarge* the harvest of your righteousness. You will be made rich in every way so that you can be generous..." (2 Corinthians 9:8,9-11).

Question: Is God *enlarging* your giving ability because you are already giving more? Remember, as you "shovel" into His bin, He will "shovel" into yours...and His "shovel" is bigger! (see Copy 2)

8. It *supports ministries.* Paul says that the Lord has commanded that those who preach the gospel should receive their living from the gospel (1 Corinthians 9:11). "I rejoice greatly in the Lord that at last you have renewed your concern for me...for even when I was in Thessalonica, you sent me aid again and again when I was in need. Not that I am looking for a gift, but I am looking for what may be credited to your account" (Philippians 4:17).

Question: Are you supporting the church and other ministries according to how God has blessed you?

Copy 9—What's the Answer?

Financial mismanagement is a leading cause of strife in families. These struggles are a result of accepting the hollow promises of materialism—and the debt that is part of seeking the so-called "good life." Jesus said in Luke 12:15, "Watch out! Be on your guard against all kinds of greed; a man's life does not consist in the abundance of his possessions."

Many of us agree there is a problem, but what is the answer? How can we experience the freedom and joy of biblical stewardship? We must start by placing our personal finances under the Lordship of Christ, being accountable to God and each other.

One excellent way to begin is through participating in one of our *Small Group Bible Studies* that deal with our finances. Or, attend our upcoming financial seminar (*put your own event info here*) Four objectives of these studies or seminars are:

1. **Encourage people to experience a more intimate fellowship with Christ.** Luke 16:11 explains the correlation between how we handle resources and our fellowship with the Lord: "So if you have not been trustworthy in handling worldly wealth, who will trust you with true riches?"

2. **Challenge each person to invite Jesus Christ to be his/her Lord.** Money may be the primary competitor with Christ for the Lordship of our lives. Matthew 6:24 reads, "No one can serve two masters. Either he will hate the one and love the other, or he will be devoted to the one and despise the other. You cannot serve both God and money."

3. **Build close relationships among the participants.**

4. **Help the students put their financial house in order.**

When you are freer to serve Christ with the resources He has entrusted to you, you will notice a greater joy and desire to participate in and give to the Lord's work. For more information about (put info here), contact the church office.

Copy 10—*God's Ownership.*[14]

Have you ever known someone who borrowed something for a long time and eventually forgot who the owner was? Or have you ever forgotten who "that borrowed book" belongs to?

In the parable of the wicked husbandmen (Matthew 21:33-41), the owner of a vineyard remained in the far country apparently for a prolonged period without requesting a progress report from the husbandmen. As time passed the husbandmen came to the conclusion that the fruit of the vineyard rightfully belonged to them.

---

[14] Dan Merkh, *TogetherWay Manual,* National Association of Freewill Baptists. Used by permission.

Just as the evil tenants attempted to take possession of the vineyard, we are prone to the same attitude. We become possessive of what God has entrusted to us. Stewardship recognizes God's ownership of all things. Colossians 1:16b clearly states that all things were created by Christ and for Himself.

Because we are not called on to give a present account of our stewardship, we are in danger of losing sight of the true owner. The longer we use God's gifts without recognizing His ownership, the more likely we will begin to view them as our rightful possessions.

The parable of the rich man in Luke 12 shows the folly of laying up treasure for ourselves and not being rich toward God. As good stewards we must continually remind ourselves of God's rightful ownership of all that we possess.

> **Question:** Do you view yourself as the rightful owner of your stuff, or God's stuff?

NOTE: More copy (19 additional) is on the Vision Resourcing Group website. Type in http://www.visionresourcinggroup.com/bookresources to access these *"Free Resources". You will be asked to setup your User Name and Password to gain instant access to these valuable resources. You can also scan the QR code posted on the first page of Appendix One with your Smart Phone which takes you directly to the "Free Resources" page.*

ARTICLES ON STEWARDSHIP

Use these articles to help you **educate your leadership team** as they implement your stewardship/generosity ministry. These can also be material for teaching your pastoral staff and organization leaders. The ones taken from materials published by the former Christian Stewardship Association (CSA), as noted, are used by permission.

Article One:[15]
Church Stewardship and Funding Trends
(Written by Brian Kluth, ex-CSA President; www.kluth.org)

Old & Ineffective Patterns	*Emerging Solutions*
Stewardship = budget, bills, buildings	**Stewardship** = a vital aspect of Christian discipleship
Focus = the church needs money	**Focus** = Christians receive biblical financial teaching
Christian Ed. = no biblical financial or stewardship teaching	**Christian Ed.** = stewardship teaching is integrated into curriculum for all ages (Sunday School, small groups, seminars)
Membership orientation = financial and giving information ignored	**Membership orientation** = financial and giving information and guidelines integrated into membership orientation and materials
Stewardship Planning = reactive to church money needs	**Stewardship Planning** = proactive stewardship teaching and initiatives woven into the church's 12-month calendar
Preaching = ignored or once-a-year stewardship message	**Preaching** = annual stewardship series and/or stewardship and financial principles woven into messages

---

[15] Brian Kluth, past president, Christian Stewardship Association. *Stewardship Resource Manual.* Used by permission.

Giving statements = sent out annually with no appreciation expressed and no accompanying information

Giving statements = mailed out quarterly with appreciation and church financial information included

Staff = stewardship is in no one's job description

Staff = lay leader(s) or associate pastor of stewardship, oversees stewardship teaching through Sunday school, small groups, seminars, spiritual gifts guidance, debt counseling; may also have responsibilities for missions, capital campaigns, and written financial communications to the congregation

Worship service = announcements are made about the church's bills, budgets, or financial shortfall

Worship service = 2-3-minute lay testimonies about how God taught people to give 10% or more; may include drama

Giving patterns = the assumption is that most people give on a weekly basis (not reality)

Giving patterns = churches offering people ways to "give" to God according to the way they "receive" from God (weekly, biweekly, monthly, send in offerings by mail, electronic funds transfer, stocks/bonds, year-end bonuses)

Church boards = faithful stewardship not a requirement to be on the church board

Church boards = faithful stewardship giving is a requirement to be on the church board

Missions = given a medium or low priority

Missions = strategic missions giving as a top priority

10% giving = 10% giving is ignored entirely or is taught as the ultimate goal to strive for someday

Business meetings = everyone given detailed financial reports that most people do not understand

Building projects = primarily paid for through mortgages or bonds

People's debt problems = the pastor and church unequipped and unprepared to handle

Career/vocational needs = completely ignored

10% giving = giving 10% or more is taught as the starting point of faithful stewardship giving

Business meetings = everyone is given financial summary pie charts and major financial goals (detailed financial reports are made available after the meeting to anyone who would like them)

Building projects = primarily or entirely paid for through organized, biblically-based giving drives with leadership gifts being given before asking the rest of the congregation to make their commitments

People's debt problems = primarily handled through small group financial Bible studies, seminars and lay debt counselors

Career/vocational needs = Christian career/vocational testing, guidance and support services

Article Two:

10 Biblical and Practical Reasons to Teach People to Give to the Lord 10% or More of Their Income: [16]

1. It is a tried and proven pattern of giving done by godly people throughout the ages regardless of cultures and income levels. (Genesis 14:17-20; 28:16-22; Leviticus 27:30; Proverbs 3:9,10; Malachi 3:7-15; Matthew 23:23)

2. It will help them reverence God more in their life. (Deuteronomy 14:23)

3. It will bring God's wisdom and order to their finances and will help harness the dragon of materialism in their life. (Matthew 6:19-21, 24-34; Luke 12:16-21; 1 Timothy 6:6-10, 17-19; Ecclesiastes 5:10)

4. It will serve as a practical reminder that God is the owner of everything in their life. (1 Chronicles 29:11-18; Psalms 24:1-2; 50:10-12; Haggai 2:8)

5. It will allow them to experience God's creative care and provision in ways they would not otherwise experience. (1 Kings 17; Proverbs 3:9-10; Malachi 3:7-15; Haggai 1:4-11; 2:15-19; Luke 6:38; Deuteronomy 28; Philippians 4:15-19; Mark 12:41-44)

6. It will encourage their spiritual growth and trust in God. Deuteronomy 14:23; Proverbs 3:5-6; Malachi 3:8-10; Haggai 1:4-11; 2:15-19; 2 Corinthians 8:5)

7. It will ensure them treasure in heaven. (1 Timothy 6:18-19; Matthew 6:19-21; Hebrews 6:10; 3 John 8; 1 Samuel 30:22)

8. It will strengthen the ministry, outreach and stability of their local church. (Acts 2:42-47; 2 Corinthians 9:12-13)

9. It will help provide the means to keep their Pastor and missionaries in full-time Christian service. (1 Corinthians 9:9-11,14; 1 Timothy 5:17-18; 3 John 5-8;

---

[16] Ibid.

Philippians 4:15-19; Galatians 6:6; Luke 8:3; 2 Kings 4:8-10)

10. **It will help accomplish needed building projects and renovations.** (2 Chronicles 24:4-14; Exodus 35 & 36; 2 Kings 12:2-16; 1 Chronicles 19:2-19; Ezekiel 1:4-6)

Article Three:

Fund-Raising Versus Stewardship—Different Approaches to Resource Development [17]

	Fund-Raising	Stewardship
Purpose	Fund the desired activity	Worship God
Goal	Meet budget; pay the bills	Serve God with full integrity
Realm of activity	Financial	Spiritual
Source of resources	Donors	God
Guiding document	Institutional budget	Bible
Motivation to give	Satisfy personal needs or emotions	Thank God; fulfill spiritual responsibility
Personal return on investment	Self-satisfaction; tax deduction	Joy of giving; blessing of obedience to God

---

[17] George Barna, *How to Increase Giving in Your Church*, page 24, Regal Books, a division of Gospel Light. Used by permission.

Precipitating relationship	Cause, institution or individual	God
Primary outcome of a donation	A better society	Bonding with God; His trust justified
Reasons for not donating	Skepticism, caution, prefer other opportunities	Ignorance of responsibility, lack of commitment to God, confusion about responsibility

Whether you choose to pursue a fund-raising approach or a stewardship approach, a key outcome of either is to secure sufficient funding to facilitate effective ministry.

NOTE: There are 3 additional articles on the Vision Resourcing Group website. Type in http://www.visionresourcinggroup.com/bookresources to access these *"Free Resources". You will be asked to setup your User Name and Password to gain instant access to these valuable resources. You can also scan the QR code posted on the first page of Appendix One with your Smart Phone which takes you directly to the "Free Resources" page.*

On the next page is a **Quit-Claim Deed** form you can make copies from to distribute to students in one of your classes or small group fellowships that are going through a stewardship teaching series. The *Crown Financial Ministries* small groups already have this form in their manuals. This would be a good form to have your people complete when you get to the lesson on God's ownership.

Quit-Claim Deed

This Quit-Claim Deed, made the _____ day of _____,

_____

FROM: _____

TO: The Lord

I (we hereby transfer to the Lord the ownership of the following possessions:

Witnesses who will help hold me (us) accountable in the recognition of God's ownership:

Stewards of the possessions above:

_____

_____

_____

Signatures

_____

_____

Signatures

QUOTES, FACTOIDS, VERSES, MISCELLANEOUS

This **section** is the final "catch-all" of information I just had to share with you! You can use these quotes, factoids, verses, and miscellaneous material in your newsletter, sermons, teaching lessons and worship service "stewardship moments." *Be creative.*

QUOTES: (My selection is from all types, Christians and non-Christians)

- "Today if you have your own home, if you have a reliable means of transportation, and if you receive an annual raise in salary, you are in the top 15% of the world's wealth. If you have two cars, two salaries, multiple changes of clothes and regular promotions, you've just jumped to the top 5% of the world's wealth...God wants to know: 'What are you complaining about?'" (Tony Evans—CSA magazine)
- "Many believers are living under a closed heaven. They pray, but the door is locked because they're robbing God (Malachi 3). If you give someone the keys to your car and this person never brings your car back, are you going to give him or her keys to your house? Not likely. In the same way, if God can't trust His children with a little, why give them more?" (Tony Evans—CSA magazine)
- "The only investments I ever made which have paid constantly increasing dividends are those I have given to the Lord's work. Pastors do their congregation a great service by helping those in the church understand God's truths about money, time and giving." (J.L. Kraft, Founder, Kraft Foods)
- "A checkbook is a theological document; it tells you who and what you worship." (Billy Graham)
- "If we really believed that our works in this life, what we do with all of our resources, will have an irreversible effect on eternity...then surely we would live differently!...Let us read our own obituary, not as written by uninformed or

biased men, but as an on looking angel might write it from heaven's point of view. Look at it carefully. Then let us use the rest of our lives to edit that obituary into what we really want it to be." (Randy Alcorn, *Money, Possessions, and Eternity*)

- "The true value of money is not in its possession, but in its use." (Aesop)
- "Tithing is not a matter of money, it is an issue of trust." (John Maxwell)
- "I have held many things in my hands and I have lost them all. But whatever I have placed in God's hands, that I still possess." (Martin Luther)
- "Indeed, if we consider the unblushing promises of rewards promised in the Gospels, it would seem that our Lord finds our desires not too strong, but too weak. We are half-hearted creatures, fooling about with drink and sex and ambition when infinite joy is offered us, like an ignorant child who wants to go on making mud pies in a slum because he cannot imagine what is meant by the offer of a holiday at the sea. We are far too easily pleased." (C.S. Lewis)
- "One more revival—only one more—is needed, the revival of Christian stewardship, the consecration of the money power to God. When that revival comes, the kingdom of God will come in a day." (Horace Bushnell)
- "True happiness comes from spiritual wealth, not material wealth." (Sir John Templeton)
- "I never would have been able to tithe on my first million dollars if I had not learned to tithe on my first paycheck, which was $1.50 for the week." (John D. Rockefeller)
- "When it comes to giving, some folks will stop at nothing." (Jimmy Carter)
- "What God orders, He pays for. Where God guides, He provides." (Anonymous)

- "We make a living through what we get; we make a life through what we give." (Winston Churchill)
- "God has given us two hands—one to receive with and the other to give with. We are not cisterns for hoarding; we are channels made for sharing." (Billy Graham)
- "It pays to serve God, but it doesn't pay to serve God because it pays." (R.G. LeTourneau)
- "Make money your god and it will plague you like the devil!" (Henry Fielding)
- "Money talks. It says, 'Good-bye.'" (Brian Kluth)
- "Christian stewardship is more than the management of things; it is the refusal to let things manage us." (James A. Lollis)
- "Don't give 'til it hurts; give 'til it feels good." (Anonymous)
- "There are three levels of giving: *you *have to* (law); *you *ought to* (obligation); *you *want to* (grace). [Waldo Werning]
- "I will place no value on anything I may possess except in relation to the kingdom of Christ. If anything I have will advance the interests of that kingdom, it shall be given away or kept, only as by giving or keeping it, I may promote the glory of Him, to Whom I owe all my hopes in time and eternity." (David Livingstone)
- "The good life exists only when you stop wanting a better one. It is the condition of savoring what is, rather than longing for what might be. The itch for things—so brilliantly injected by those who make and sell them—is in effect a virus draining the soul of contentment. A man never earns enough, a woman is never beautiful enough, clothes are never new enough, the house is never furnished enough, the food is never fancy enough. There is a point at which salvation lies in stepping off the escalator, of saying, "Enough: What I have will do, what I make of it is up to me." (Marya Mannes—Reader's Digest, *Points to Ponder)*

- "The person who dedicates his money to God is dedicating himself—the fruit of his time, talent and energy. One who fails to dedicate his money has not fully committed himself to God." (Anonymous)

NOTE: There are 76 additional "quotes" on the Vision Resourcing Group website. Type in http://www.visionresourcinggroup.com/bookresources to access these *"Free Resources". You will be asked to setup your User Name and Password to gain instant access to these valuable resources. You can also scan the QR code posted on the first page of Appendix One with your Smart Phone which takes you directly to the "Free Resources" page.*

A FEW FACTOIDS

- "The United States possesses 5% of the world's population, but possesses 85-90% of the world's *Christian* wealth."
- Among church members of 11 primary Protestant denominations (or their historical antecedents) in the United States and Canada, per-member giving as a percentage of income was lower in 2000 than in either 1921 or 1933. In 1921, per-member giving as a percentage of income was 2.9 percent. In 1933, at the depth of the Great Depression, per-member giving grew to 3.3 percent. By 2000, after a half-century of unprecedented prosperity, giving had fallen to 2.6 percent. Currently it has remained less than 3 percent.
- Overall, only 3 to 5 percent of Americans who donate money to a church tithe (give a tenth of) their incomes, though many more claim to do so.
- If members of historically Christian churches in the United States raised their giving to a tithe (10% of income) in 2000, an additional $139 billion a year would become available. That potential has increased sizably today.

- Stewardship of money: one-third of Jesus' parables; the second-most-frequently discussed subject in the ministry of Christ (next to teaching of the kingdom).
- Harvard University economist Juliet Schor found that for every hour of television watched per week, annual spending increased $208.
- According to some statistics that his firm had gathered in the United Kingdom, Richard J. Radcliffe, Chairman of Smee and Ford in the UK, reported that the average age of people dying without a will was 69; the average age of people dying with a will was 79, and the average age of people dying with a will AND with a charitable bequest was 82. (Is there a connection here?)

SOME SCRIPTURE REFERENCES

General: 1 Chronicles 29:11-14; Psalm 50:10-12; Haggai 1:6-9; 2:8; 1 Corinthians 4:2,7; James 1:17; Romans 11:36; Acts 17:24, 25, 28; 2 Corinthians 5:14-15; Luke 16:1-2, 10-13; Romans 14:12: Leviticus 19:11: Colossians 3:23-24; Mark 8:36

Borrowing: Exodus 22:14; Deuteronomy 15:1-11; Psalm 37:25; Proverbs 3:27-28; 22:7; Matthew 5:25-26, 40; 18:23-35; Luke 12:58-59

Contentment: Psalm 119:14, 57, 72; Proverbs 3:13; 8:18-21; 10:22; Matthew 20:1-16; Luke 3:14; Philippians 4:11-14; Colossians 3:2; 1 Thessalonians 5:18; 1 Timothy 3:3; 6:6-10; Hebrews 13:5; 1 John 2:15

Cosigning: Proverbs 6:1; 11:15; 17:18; 19:19; 20:16; 22:26-27

Counsel: Proverbs 12:5; 12:15; 13:20; 14:7, 15; 15:22; 19:20; 24:6; 27:9

Debt: Deuteronomy 15:6; 2 Kings 4:1; Psalm 37:21; Proverbs 3:27-28; 22:7; Romans 13:8

Giving: Genesis 28:13, 20, 22; Exodus 23:19; 25:1-2; Leviticus 27:30,32; Numbers 18:29-30, 32; Deuteronomy 14:23; 15:7-8;

16:16,17; 1 Chronicles 29:9, 11-18; Nehemiah 8:10; Psalm 37:21; Proverbs 3:9-10; 11:24-26; 21:25-26; 25:21,22; 28:27; Malachi 3:8-10; Matthew 6:1-4; 25:31,34-37,40; Luke 6:38; 14:13,14; 21:1-4; Acts 2:44-45; 20:33-35; 4:32-35; Romans 12:6,8,13; 1 Corinthians 9:11,14; 16:1-2; 2 Corinthians 8-9; Galatians 6:6, 9-10; Ephesians 4:28; Philippians 4:14-19; 1 Timothy 6:17-19; Hebrews 13:16; 1 John 3:17-18;

God's giving: James 1:5; 1 Timothy 6:17; Psalm 103:2-4; 147:5,8,9,14; Acts 14:17; Matthew 5:45; 1 John 4:10; Romans 5:8; 8:32; John 3:16; 1 Timothy 2:6; Galatians 2:20; Titus 2:14; 2 Peter 1:3,4; 2 Corinthians 8:9; 9:8, 15.

Greed: Proverbs 21:17; 22:16; 23:6-7; Ecclesiastes 5:10, 13; Matthew 6:19,24; 19:23; Luke 9:25; 12:15-21; Acts 5:1-10; Ephesians 5:5; Colossians 3:5; 1 Timothy 6:10; James 3:14-16; 4:3

Inheritance: Proverbs 13:22; 17:2; 20:21; Ecclesiastes 2:18-19, 21; Luke 15:11-31

Investments: Psalm 62:10; 127:1-2; Proverbs 11:28; 21:5; 23:4-5; 24:27; 28:20-22; Matthew 6:19-21; 25:14-29; Luke 19:12-26; 2 Timothy 2:4

Saving: Proverbs 6:6-10; 21:5, 20; Matthew 6:19-20

Time & Talent: Ecclesiastes 3:1-8; Ephesians 5:15-17; Psalm 90:12; Exodus 36:1; 1 Peter 4:10-11; Ephesians 2:20; 2:10; Luke 12:19-20; Philippians 2:4; Isaiah 48:17; 1 Corinthians 12:7; Proverbs 16:9; 6:6-11

True Riches: James 2:5; Hebrews 11:24-26; Philippians 3:7-8; Matthew 6:19-21; 1 Timothy 6:17-19; Psalm 16:11; Proverbs 8:17-21; 10:22; Revelations 2:9; Ephesians 1:18; Colossians 1:27; 1 Peter 1:3-9

Wealth: Deuteronomy 8:18; Proverbs 23:4-5; Luke 12:16-21

MISCELLANEOUS

Some additional TIPS on raising funds for your vision and ministry:

1. Plan an "All-church Tithing Sunday," where you challenge your congregation, in advance, to bring a tithe of their gross monthly income on that special Sunday. It will reveal the real potential of giving if everyone tithed. An alternative approach is to ask them to write down on a slip of paper, anonymously, what their tithe amount would be if they tithed the full 10%. Compute the total and report the results to the congregation. Chances are you and they will be shocked!

2. Schedule a *Missions Month,* or *Building Month,* or *Give It Away Month* for special offerings. Don't do this too often.

3. Repeatedly share your vision for ministry through all avenues. People want to be part of something bigger than themselves.

4. Manage well your donor records in order to spot the spiritual health of your people.

5. Send out *Thank You* letters, including ministry updates, testimonials, financial reports and vision casting.

6. Make *Thank You* phone calls to your consistent givers. Cast vision, take prayer requests, ask questions. Divide this task among staff and key leaders, and don't limit these calls only to your big givers. You want to encourage your small, but consistent, givers.

7. Communicate to your members and, in particular, your leaders that as part of their discipleship they are expected to give to church ministry.

NOTE: There are 5 additional "Miscellaneous" items on the Vision Resourcing Group website. Type in http://www.visionresourcinggroup.com/bookresources to access these *"Free Resources". You will be asked to setup your User Name and Password to gain instant access to these valuable resources. You can also scan the QR code posted on the first page of Appendix One with your Smart Phone which takes you directly to the "Free Resources" page.*

APPENDIX TWO

Resources offered by our Vision Resourcing Group *Consultants* utilizing our Partners and our Associate Organizations, plus a list of miscellaneous organizations, literature, books, and specialized consultants.

There are many resources "out there" to draw from for stewardship/generosity ministry help and information. There are non-profit organizations that provide studies and educational material, and there are professional consultants, books, videos, newsletters and other publications. This is an alphabetical listing of a *limited* selection to assist you and save you time in researching and choosing what additional resources might be of help to you.

VISION RESOURCING GROUP

In my opinion, **your first choice** should be to call **VISION RESOURCING GROUP** and have them do a *profile survey*. This will *help you decide* which direction to proceed and which resources you should consider for your unique needs and goals. Here is some information about us:

We are a group of consultants and trainers passionate about helping the body of Christ grow more into mature biblical stewards and generous givers. Our strategy is to focus our efforts on Christian leaders, training them to be able to lead, teach and train their congregations and people within their sphere of influence toward a culture of biblical leadership, stewardship and generosity. We are equipped with many resources, both our own, and from our partner ministries, to provide solutions for our client organizations, whether they are churches, denominations, Para-church ministries, businesses, or schools.

Our *vision* is: *"To see Christian leaders equipped in training others to become more generous givers and faithful managers of God's resources."*

We are guided in our ministry by Ephesians 4:12-13, "To prepare God's people so that the body of Christ may be built up until all….become mature, attaining to the whole measure of Christ."

Utilizing our "Consult-Equip-Support" process, our primary objective is to "train the trainer". We meet with you to determine your goals and needs, help you develop a tailored action plan, equip you with selected resources, and follow up in supporting you toward success. You can reach us at www.visionresourcinggroup.com, call us at 949.916.7560, or email us at info@visionresourcinggroup.com. We look forward to helping resource your vision.

The following flow-chart describes our process of working with a client church:

THE CHURCHES STEWARDSHIP
SOLUTION
Creating a culture of stewardship and generosity

VISION RESOURCING GROUP
CONSULT - EQUIP - SUPPORT

1 CONSULT

Discover
Prayer
Ask - Listen
Learn

Analyze
Identify
Strengths
Needs & Goals

Blue Print
Develop a custom
action
Plan - Prayer

Convenant
Choose an option
Mutually agree

2 EQUIP

Team Development
Train Leaders on Team Role

Implement
Integrate action plan and education
curriculum

3 SUPPORT

Manage
Financial Reports
Team Meetings
Accountibility

Celebration
Results
Evaluations yearly

(949) 916 - 7560   www.VisionResourcingGroup.com

VISION RESOURCING GROUP *PARTNERS*

WE ARE A *CERTIFIED* PROVIDER OF CONSULTING, TRAINING AND SUPPORTING FOR OUR PARTNER CONTENT. YOU CAN CONTACT VISION RESOURCING GROUP (VRG) FOR MORE INFORMATION.

1. **VRG** uses **BPFL's** content, a 10-part interactive study for individuals and groups, to help your people discover the life purpose that God intended for them. Pursuing God's dream for their life is not a matter of pushing themselves

harder, but of allowing God to pull them toward the life that has been quietly calling from within all along. BPFL helps them identify and design a strategic life plan—a personal blueprint for their life —and create intentional action steps to experience the life they were born to live in five major areas of life: Spiritual, Relational, Physical, Financial and Career. They will discover the life they were born to live.

2. **VRG** uses **C– FGW** to teach people of all ages how to handle money based on the principles of the bible. We do this through their menu of written materials in hard copy and online electronic format.

3. **VRG** uses **CI of E** material to provide a small group, workshop, or interactive seminar "The 10", to help organizations enhance the moral character and decision making process of their people. As organizations grow, the ability to maintain an integrity-based culture becomes increasingly difficult. This training will help reinforce your organization's values.

4. **VRG** uses **C** small group and seminar material to equip people in your organization to learn, apply, and teach biblical financial principles so that they may know Christ more intimately, be free to serve Him, and help fund the Great Commission. They do this through a menu of teaching resources for all ages and walks of life.

5. **VRG** uses **EPL** materials to enable leaders to achieve performance excellence through the integration of biblical principles and leadership strategies and skills. Through their workshops and website, they help leaders integrate their faith and their work.

6. **VRG** connects you to **GC's** *online learning* system which is a cutting-edge way for you, your leadership teams, and your people grow in their knowledge of the biblical message of generosity, anywhere anytime. Each option (a six-week training for your leaders & a four-week training for your attendees) provides an experience filled with daily

activities that combine the same things you do every day on the web – read, watch videos, and blog or journal. The result? A fun, interactive way to nurture a culture of generosity in your church or organization.

7. **VRG** uses **PDP'S** workshops and one on one coaching assessments to help organizations bring out the best in people at every level, from the executive team to line staff and volunteers. Their TeamScan helps you create effective teams and work groups by providing objective measurements and narrative reporting of group characteristics including resolving interpersonal conflicts.

8. **VRG** uses **T-1 TECHNOLOGY** that offers industry-leading volunteer and employee background screening solutions that can be tailored to your organization's culture. In addition, educational online training and testing can be customized for your specific needs.

9. **VRG partners with BRIAN KLUTH's – MAXIMUM GENEROSITY** ministry materials and speaking resources to help your organization "maximize" its generosity teaching to your people. His "40 Day Spiritual Journey to a More Generous Life" Bible devotional has 500,000 copies in print, and has been used by hundreds of churches to inspire greater generosity and increased giving for general offerings and/or building-fund campaigns. We are able to schedule him to speak at local, regional and denominational church and Para-church seminars and conferences.

10. **VRG** partners with an organization that helps churches and ministries be more effective and efficient in utilizing technology. An example is their Bible Study Connection, a web-based platform that organizations can use to train and disciple people online. The tool connects people in an online study environment, with class information, forums, chats, and a live conferencing experience. This replicates the in-person small group or bible study experience. Any content can be used and taught through this multi-lingual platform.

11. **VRG** provides its own Budget Coach Training, designed to equip and prepare individuals and couples as a budget coach. When the training is completed, they will be able to assist folks with analyzing their current situation, help them develop a workable budget, prepare a debt retirement strategy and begin both short and long term savings plans. They will also be able to help business owners separate their personal finances from their business finances.

12. **VRG** partners with K.S., and his Financial Wellness Curriculum. This teaching curriculum is designed specifically for the business secular environment, teaching employees how to manage their finances, reduce debt, save, and basically reduce their financial stress that affects their productivity at work. The business leader can choose between using biblical principles without the bible passages being mentioned or using a curriculum utilizing biblical passages. This can be a win-win opportunity for the employer and employee.

13. **VRG** partners with **SM** and their teaching resources, including many short videos assessable on our website. We, along with their videos and material, are committed to helping believers understand and apply the truths of God's ownership, transforming every area of your people's lives – home, careers and church.

14. **VRG** partners with **Good $ense Stewardship Ministry.** Formerly a ministry of the Willow Creek Association, they have excellent stewardship training studies to guide you in teaching your congregation or membership in budgeting, debt reduction and biblical principles of money management. They also provide training conferences, Good $ense counselor training, and personal budgeting workshops for churches. You can contact them through VRG.

VRG ASSOCIATES –

Other organizations we draw from to help our clients succeed:

1. **CHARITABLE GIVING FOUNDATION** has created a wonderful program where you can purchase quality products and services from a pre-screened group of businesses called **'Inner Circle' members,** who will give back a portion of the purchase price to the Charitable Giving Foundation. Our Foundation in turn makes a contribution to the *purchaser`s* favorite cause, `Select Group` member or one of our `Approved Organizations`. This is a win-win opportunity for all. To learn more, click on http://www.charitablegivingfoundation.org/dotnetnuke/AboutUs.aspx.

2. **CHRISTIAN FOUNDATION OF THE WEST** (CFW) was established to help donors, churches, ministries and professional advisors promote *Smart Giving.* Through the foundations charitable tools, services and expert counsel, CFW helps support a broad range of ministries, by making it possible for people to give in ways many they never imagined. To learn more click on http://cfwest.com/.

3. **CRESCENDO INTERACTIVE** is the largest provider of planned giving solutions, having grown to over 9,000+ client licenses. Their mission is to provide non-profit organizations with comprehensive, flexible solutions that help their donors make planned gifts. To learn more, click on http://www.crescendointeractive.com.

4. **EVANGELICAL CHRISTIAN CREDIT UNION** is the leading banking resource for growing churches, Christian schools, and other evangelical ministries. More than 8,000 people, including 3,500 missionaries in more than 100 countries, also trust ECCU for their banking needs. Individuals who bank with ECCU appreciate the fact that their deposits are used exclusively to resource evangelical ministries. To learn more, click on https://www.eccu.org/.

5. **KINGDOM ADVISERS** exists to encourage, educate, and empower Christian financial professionals to be effective disciples of Jesus Christ so that they can provide professional counsel from a biblical wisdom perspective to their clients. All Qualified Kingdom Advisors have completed the Kingdom Advisors Core Training and met certain criteria before being available as referred financial professionals to interested clients. To learn more, click on http://www.kingdomadvisors.org/getstarted.asp.

6. **NATIONAL CHRISTIAN FOUNDATION & WATER-STONE FOUNDATION** are mentioned in my section on estate and gift planning.

7. **TURNING POINT STEWARDSHIP** is a full service for-profit consulting firm that partners with local churches to provide their people professional Christian counseling in the area of marriages, debt consolidation, financial planning, tax planning and a unique capability for families to manage their cash and pay their bills. They undergird all of their services using biblical principles. To learn more, click on www.turningpointstewardship.com, or call 800.296.5899.

8. **VISION'S INTERNATIONAL TRAINING AND EDUCATION NETWORK** (ITEN) is a school of ministry and consortium of bible college and university programs, with mentorship in and through local churches. VIEN seeks to emphasize the practical aspects of ministry service. They actively partner with established church-based training programs and schools of ministry around the globe. They help local churches establish their own School of Ministry, called "Learning Centers" in order to provide advanced and credited biblical training to their members and community. To learn more, click on www.vienetwork.net/.

SOME ADDITIONAL "OUTSIDE" RESOURCES

1. **American Church Stewardship Resources.** They provide offering envelope services and *Electronic Church Giving,* which is an electronic funds transfer service for members to make biweekly, monthly or quarterly contributions to your church. If your church is comfortable offering this service to your people, this is the place to call. They take care of the processing. Their phone number is (800) 446-3035, and their website is http://www.americanchurch.com/.

2. **Christian Credit/Debt Financial Counseling agencies.** There are service agencies in all 50 states and major metropolitan cities, providing assistance in eliminating credit debt. They counsel people in financial and debt management, setting them up on a debt payoff program. They arrange with creditors for interest rate and payment reduction, and put the debtors on an arranged, fixed monthly payment that fits within their budget. There is usually **no** charge to the client. However, they may ask them to make a monthly donation to their non-profit organization to help defray their costs of operation. The agencies usually receive financial help from the credit card companies. Currently, these Christian credit counseling agencies are limited to only serving those geographical areas where they have counselor staff, because of the requirement of having to provide optional face-to-face counseling. Separate agencies cannot be listed here for all states and large cities, but you can search the Internet for the names and phone numbers in your area.

3. **Dave Ramsey** has multiple resources on leadership, stewardship, money management through his books, live presentations, Financial Peace University, and debt reduction. The best way to learn more and access his resources is through his website at www.daveramsey.com.

4. **Generous Giving.** This is a supporting 501(c)3 organization established by the Maclellan Foundation. Their purpose is to provide information, tools, services, conferences and on-line content that will "transform hearts and minds for revolutionary stewardship." They offer many excellent written, audio, and video resources, including hundreds of sermons on stewardship and giving topics. Their www.generousgiving.org website is the Internet's largest known Christian stewardship library. They also offer a *Generous Church Toolkit* that provides churches the tools for a month-long campaign teaching their people to become generous givers. It includes sermons, illustrations, multi-media tools, devotional materials, Sunday school or small group study materials, audio testimonies of generous givers and a copy of Randy Alcorn's best-selling book *The Treasure Principle.* Their home office address is 820 Broad Street, Suite 300, Chattanooga, TN, 37402. Their phone number is (423) 755-2399.

5. **LifeWay Church Resources.** This is part of the Southern Baptist Convention. This is a rich source of information on a whole range of materials for a church stewardship training process. They have many printed and video resources on stewardship education, capital fundraising, financial planning, small groups and guides for leadership. Their address is LifeWay Christian Resources, One LifeWay Plaza, Nashville, TN, 37234. You can reach them at (800) 458-2772, or by their e-mail address at customerservice@lifeway.com, or their website at http://www.lifeway.com/Keyword/stewardship+resources.

6. **PhilanthroCorp.** They are a fee-only, planned giving *outsourced* company. They can help expand an existing planned giving program, or establish a new one. They can work directly with your potential donors, or train you to do it. Since most churches do not have a planned giving capability, this company can "act" as their planned giving department if they do not have access to a denominational

planned giving service. They also offer a web-based planned giving system for churches. You can reach them at 111 South Tejon, Suite 520, Colorado Springs, CO, 80903, or call them at (800) 876-7958. Their website is www.pcxhome.com.

7. **Rick Warren's www.pastors.com ministry.** Rick is the founding pastor of Saddleback Church in Lake Forest, California. He is the author of *The Purpose-Driven Church* and *Purpose-Driven Life* and has trained thousands of pastors worldwide in conferences and seminars. Rick has several stewardship messages, some of which are on PowerPoint, and he has a capital campaign program available called *Building for Life Campaign Kit.* Their address is 1 Saddleback Parkway, Lake Forrest, CA, 92630. The phone number is (949) 609-8000. Their websites are www.saddleback.com and www.purposedriven.com.

8. **Sound Mind Investing.** They exist to help individuals understand and apply biblically-based principles for making spending and investing decisions. Author and investment counselor Austin Pryor heads up this ministry/practice. His key book is *Sound Mind Investing.* One can become a member of their monthly newsletter and website sources for an annual fee. Their website is www.soundmindinvesting.com.

LITERATURE AND BOOKS

There are so many good books and literature on stewardship and generosity that I have decided to list only a selection. You obviously can contact the organizations listed here for their lists and catalogs and search other lists on websites. One of the best websites for this is Generous Giving. Visit Christian bookstores and contact publishers for additional choices. Here is my selection:

1. *44 Ways to Expand the Financial Base of Your Congregation* by L.E. Schaller (1989), Abingdon Press.

2. *1,000 Bright Ideas to Stretch Your Dollars* by Cynthia Yates, published by *Servant Publications.*
3. *Behind the Stained Glass Windows* by John & Sylvia Ronsvalle (1996), Baker Book House Co.
4. *A Biblical Theology of Material Possessions* by G.A. Getz (1990), Moody Press.
5. *The Debt Squeeze: How Your Family Can Become Financially Free* by Ron Blue.
6. *Developing a Giving Church* by Stan Toler & Elmer Towns, Beacon Hill Press, Kansas City, Mo. ISBN 083-411-7738. It is filled with great stories and examples of stewardship issues in a church. It gives guidance to church leaders for shaping a giving environment, insights from respected leaders, counsel on stewardship strategies, stewardship sermons, anecdotes, and quotes.
7. *Generous Living: Finding Contentment Through Giving* by Ron Blue. All church leaders should read this book.
8. *Generous People: How to Encourage Vital Stewardship* by Eugene Grimm (1992), Abingdon Press. ISBN: 0-687-14045-5
9. *God & Your Stuff—The Vital Link Between Your Possessions and Your Soul* by Dr. Wesley K. Wilmer; published by NAVPRESS. Dr. Wilmer is Vice President of University Advancement and a professor at Biola University.
10. *Gift of a Lifetime: Planned Giving in Congregational Life* by J. Gregory Pope; published by Broadman & Holman, Nashville, TN. ISBN 0-8054-1848-2. This book teaches how to develop a comprehensive planned giving program for your church. In addition to telling you why to do it and how to do it, it explains what planned gifts are and how to promote a planned giving program. It provides valuable helps and tools in its Appendices, including a list of resources for the task.
11. *Giving and Stewardship in an Effective Church* by Kennon L. Callahan. This book presents a practical plan for the

growth and development of giving and stewardship in a church, complete with action worksheets. Dr. Callahan is a consultant to churches and the author of several books relating to church leadership and finances.

12. *How to Increase Giving in Your Church* by George Barna. This is a practical guide to the sensitive task of raising money for your church and ministry. George Barna is founder and president of Barna Research Group, Ltd., a full-service research company. He is the author of several best-selling books. The publisher is Regal Books, a Division of Gospel Light.

13. *Master Your Money* by Ron Blue. This is his classic book that gives a step-by-step plan for financial freedom.

14. *Minister's Guide for Income Tax* by Conrad Teitell is published every year. It is published by Philanthropy Tax Institute, 13 Arcadia Road, P.O. Box 299, Old Greenwich, CT, 06870.

15. *Money, Possessions and Eternity* by Randy Alcorn, Tyndale House Publishers, Inc. This classic gives a balanced survey of the Bible's philosophy of wealth as it relates to eternity and provides help to the pastor who wants to teach his people stewardship principles. This should be the first book all of your stewardship leader team should read. It is foundational.

16. *Revolution in Generosity – Transforming Stewards to be Rich Toward God, edited by Dr. Wesley K. Willmer, Moody Press.* It calls for a paradigm shift in how God wants us to raise funds for ministry, including the church.

17. *The Pastor's Guide to Fund-Raising Success* by Dr. Dorsey E. Levell & Wayne E. Groner (1999), Bonus Books, Inc. They provide experienced and practical helps on conducting annual stewardship drives and capital funds campaigns.

18. *Saving Money Any Way You Can: How to Become a Frugal Family* by Mike Yorkey. You can purchase this at your Christian bookstore.

19. *Stewards in the Kingdom* by R. Scott Rodin, InterVarsity Press (2000). The kingdom concept forms the backbone of his treatment of stewardship as a lifestyle, recognizing the fact that the Christian belongs to God's kingdom alone, not also to the world's kingdom. While he deals with the financial side of stewardship, he does so only after a thorough exploration of the real identity of the steward functioning within God's kingdom.

20. *The Treasure Principle—Discovering The Secret of Joyful Giving* by Randy Alcorn, Multnomah Publishers. This is a small book all your leaders should read.

21. *Using Your Money Wisely* by Larry Burkett. A practical guide to personal money management. It would be good for your church library.

22. *The Word on Finances* by Larry Burkett. This book is filled with topical Scriptures and commentary.

23. *The Worshipgiver: One Who Gives as an Expression of Worship* by Talmage Williams. He has served as director of stewardship development at the Baptist State Convention of North Carolina, through which you can obtain the book. You can also get a copy through LifeWay Church Resources, listed above. The book talks about "worship and giving" and "how to make giving worshipful." This book would be useful for your stewardship "moments" prior to taking offerings.

24. *Building Your Church: Using Your Gifts, Time and Resources,* 13 studies by Don Cousins and Judson Poling with contributions from Bruce Bugbee and Bill Hybels. This study guide is part of the Willow Creek Resources and is published by Zondervan Publishing House.

25. *Jesus on MONEY?* by Kay Moore, based on Larry Burkett's book *Using Your Money Wisely.* Three six-week courses published by LifeWay Church Resources. Their website is www.lifeway.com. Their phone number is (800) 458-2772.

26. *Mastering Money* by Dudley Delffs. This is a *Pilgrimage Small Group Guide* published by NavPress, Colorado Springs, CO. There are eight study sessions.

RESOURCES FOR CAPITAL FUND CAMPAIGNS

Your denominational service center, if you have one, is a good place to start looking for help. If you are not part of a denomination, there are many resources to consider. Here are a few:

1. As mentioned above, Rick Warren's ministry to pastors and churches, www.pastors.com, offers their *Building for Life Campaign Kit*, which has been used by Rick's church and many other churches to raise millions of dollars for capital building projects. You can order the kit through his website.

2. *Cargill Associates.* This is a professional consulting firm that offers counsel on capital fund raising for churches. You can reach them at 4701 Altamesa Blvd, P.O. Box 330339, Fort Worth, TX, 76163-0339, or call them at (800) 433-2233. The Fax number is (817) 292-9631. Their website address is www.cargillassociates.com. They have an outline named *Steps to a Successful Church Capital Funds Drive.*

3. *The Timothy Group.* This professional consulting agency provides comprehensive assistance in stewardship development, including capital fund campaigns for churches. You can reach them at 1663 Sutherland Drive, S.E., Grand Rapids, MI 49508-4904, or call them at (616) 224-4060, or visit their website at www.timothygroup.com.

4. *The INJOY* GROUP. One of their services is their INJOY Stewardship Services, consulting with churches in raising capital funds. You can reach them at P.O. Box 2782, Suwanee, GA 30024, or call them at 800.333.6506 or visit them at their website, www.injoy.com.

5. The Goehner Group. Mentioned above, they provide consulting services in capital fund campaigns. You can reach them at 4125 Blackford Ave., Suite 205, San Jose, CA, 95117-1705, or call them at (408) 246-6002, or visit their website at www.goehnergroup.com.
6. *Building God's Way.* This is a building design and Service Company that helps churches and Christian schools save up to 60% on their building costs. They provide training, resources and expertise in affordable building design and construction. They have a unique system of building. You can reach them at 1661 West 2750 South, Ogden, Utah, 84401, or phone them at (800) 800.552.7137, or visit their website at www.buildinggodsway.com.
7. **Books on Capital Campaigns**
   - *When Not to Build: An Architect's Unconventional Wisdom for the Growing Church*, by Ray Bowman with Eddy Hall (1995).
   - *Conducting a Successful Capital Campaign* by Kent Dove (1991).
   - *Capital Campaigns* by Andrea Kihlstedt and Catherine P. Schwartz (1997).

And, finally, let me know how you are doing so that we at Vision Resourcing Group can help and/or pass it on to other Christian leaders working their stewardship/generosity ministries. Just e-mail your thoughts, experiences and suggestions to info@visionresourcinggroup.com, or myself at dedic@visionresourcinggroup.com. Also, introduce us to your other Christian leader friends you think would be interested in exploring how to implement a stewardship/generosity ministry and develop a culture of generosity to those people within their sphere of influence.

Thanks so much!

ABOUT THE AUTHOR

Dick Edic is President and Co-Founder of Vision Resourcing Group, a stewardship and generosity consulting and training ministry to Christian leaders in churches, businesses, and schools. VRG started years ago as Vision Resourcing, utilizing Dick's Training Workshop and consulting to church leaders. His primary tool for this training was his Training Kit, *Resourcing Your Vision – A Church Stewardship Ministry Guide.* This *Guide* was divided into an "Implementation Guide" and a "Resources Guide". This book, *How to Resource Your Vision,* is the rewrite of the original Training Kit. Vision Resourcing Group is the "merge" of Dick's VR ministry and Jim Sullivan's Crown Financial Ministry. VRG expands the reach of both Dick's and Jim's ministry from just church leaders to Christian leaders in business, Para-church ministries and schools. It also expands the scope of the resources they offer to include *"Consulting-Equipping-Supporting"* clients in the areas of *"providing tailored training and guidance for Christian Leaders – to enable them to better develop a culture of biblical stewardship, leadership and generosity to those people within their sphere of influence."* Through the utilization of VRG's internal, partner, and associate resources, our primary objective is to "Train the Trainer" through our consulting, equipping and supporting process.

Dick is the former Assistant to the President, Ministry Partner Services, of the Baptist General Conference (now *CONVERGE*). In that capacity, he was responsible for development, planned giving and stewardship education efforts for Baptist General Conference churches in the southwest region of the United States. He served in this position for ten years.

Dick is an Advanced Certified Stewardship Executive (A.C.S.E.) with the former Christian Stewardship Association, the stewardship arm of the National Association of Evangelicals.

He ran his own financial planning practice for ten years, and in 1986 was ranked in the top four percent nationally with a leading financial planning firm. During his three years as a real estate agent and broker, he earned the #1 salesman spot in the first year with a company that was #10 in the state of Hawaii.

He served ten years in the campus ministry of Campus Crusade for Christ, where he met and married Carolyn. They have one son, Matthew, married to Teresa, who provided a wonderful grandson and granddaughter, Will and Grace.

Dick and Carolyn live in the San Diego, California area. He enjoys a "reasonable" game of golf, handyman projects, and walking on the beach with Carolyn.